Basketball's Destroyer Offense

BASKETBALL'S DESTROYER OFFENSE

by DAYTON M. SPAULDING

Parker Publishing Company, Inc.
West Nyack, New York

© 1972 BY

PARKER PUBLISHING COMPANY, INC.
WEST NYACK, NEW YORK

LIBRARY OF CONGRESS
CATALOG CARD NUMBER: 73-184570

PRINTED IN THE UNITED STATES OF AMERICA
ISBN 0-13-056390-0
BC

DEDICATION

—to the young men who have played for me . . . to my wife Conchita and our three children, Christopher, Deborah and Michelle . . . to the many friends in Panama, Brazil and especially Spain . . . to my brother and sisters who have always cared, no matter what my venture . . . to Clair Bee and Bruce Drake who influenced my life so greatly . . . and to my mother and father who have had such abundant love that my inabilities, to some degree, have been made less noticeable.

Foreword

As coaches, we quite often tend to become dogmatic in our thinking regardless of the changing complexion of the game of basketball. But Dayton Spaulding represents one of those innovative coaches who pursues ideas which might give his team "the winning edge." His latest innovation, "The Destroyer Offense," eliminates one of the most formidable obstacles his team and all teams encounter—the zone pressure defenses.

Borrowing a page from the concepts of football coaching, this dynamic offense defeats the press in the same manner that the screen pass defeats the "blitz." The hub of the offense exists in the passing game, where passing accuracy and floor position key success. Description of the offensive attack continues beyond the "ideal" passes and alignments to include those complements necessary for its proper execution in the overall game plan, both offensively and defensively.

These complements are presented in developmental gradations which depict actual on-the-floor implementation of the offensive system. In addition to utilizing options of "The Destroyer Offense" against defensive variations, the system converts to the "Destroyer Set" offense once the ball penetrates front-court. This set incorporates offensive patterns that have proven to be the very essence of offensive basketball.

One of the most significant contributions of this book to existing basketball theory pertains to the statement, "It is impossible to have a break in the action between operating an offense and organizing to play defense if you want to be a consistent winner." All phases of "The Destroyer" and "Destroyer Set" consider the spontaneous conversion to defense and vice versa. This cycle concept should be invaluable in coaching overall understanding of the game to your players.

Dayton has enlightened offensive thinking with "The Destroyer Offense," and concurrently, he has delved into the realm of spontaneous transition from offense to defense. Although the supplemental topics discussed deserve merit, such as the mental approach to foul shooting, this progressive offensive system and its conversion represent one of "the winning edges." As a refreshing innovation, "Destroyer Offense" is a successful weapon against the increasingly popular zone presses.

Ray Mears
Head Basketball Coach
The University of Tennessee

What This Book Reveals

This book tells how a coach who believes in disciplined, patterned offenses has been able to use them with success despite zone pressure defenses. The book reveals, for the first time, a completely new offense which wipes out the effectiveness of zone presses. The author calls the offense the "Destroyer," and it has been tested in the New England State College Athletic Conference with complete success. As it is outlined in this book, it is completely new and unseen—unseen in its entirety simply because we have never had to use the complete offense to achieve the objective of its intended use. It has been used by several small college coaches. It has been used by some of our former players, such as Carl McAllister of Fall Mountain High School and Jim Krug of St. Thomas High School, quite successfully in New Hampshire High School competition.

I think this offense will take the bite out of zone pressing defenses; so much so that in neutralizing the zone presses, the game may return, in the discussion of what to stress, offense or defense, to a more balanced formula. It has never been seen on a television screen. It has never been filmed. It has never been presented at any clinic. To my knowledge there are three men, other than Plymouth State players of very recent years, who are aware of this offense. It may stimulate further discussion of the question of whether to use a 24- or a 30-second clock in the game or not. The author certainly hopes no time limit for possession of the ball will ever be the case in amateur play. But perhaps this is another matter for another book. I believe the "Destroyer" is even more startling than Coach Bruce Drake's use of ball movement in back of the base line after a field goal, when it was used for the first time many years ago by the University of Oklahoma. The word "Destroyer" is a candid term as it was used by our players, who repeatedly said, "It destroyed their press." So the term stuck. This offense functions against any zone press with amazing simplicity. So well does it function that at times just one pass causes the opposition to abandon their zone press. This has minimized scrutiny of the offense by our opponents. Recently I revealed the offense to Coach Ray Mears of Tennessee, Coach Tom Greene of Florida Southern and Coach Ed Kassler of Oneonta State. I felt these three coaches were not only amazed with the simplicity of it but also became struck with the inevitable effect it would have on zone presses.

Although I believe the highlight of the book is this offense, if indeed there is a highlight, I feel it is necessary to explain other thoughts about other phases of the game which have enabled our teams to play patterned basketball successfully. Some other ideas presented which will assure success for the coach who wants to use patterned offenses are:

(1) Defensive ideas and drills which lead to getting the ball more often.

(2) The "Destroyer" set which will score points.

(3) Definitive ideas about the development of excellent shooting performances.

In my opinion there are few or no secrets in the game. As has been said so many times, winning depends on the soundness of execution of the game's fundamentals. I certainly subscribe to that statement; nevertheless, the Destroyer Offense exists as a new innovation. At least I have never seen nor heard anything similar to this offense. Humbly I tell you that the coach who is unaware of it will be spending time for naught if he practices zone presses and his opponent uses the "Destroyer."

"Destroyer" comes from a coach who is tucked away in the hills of New Hampshire. Ideas have a way, however, of disrespecting geographic location. It does come from a coach with a winning record. It does come from a coach who has been limited to minimal recruiting. And finally, I am sure the offense had its seed bed in the mind of a *maestro*, the originator of the original "Shuffle Offense," Coach Bruce Drake of Norman, Oklahoma.

Dayton M. Spaulding

CONTENTS

Foreword 7

What This Book Reveals 9

Part I
An Offense for the Future

1. How to Put Together the Destroyer Offense 21

    Understanding the Background of the Offense (22)
    Ideas About Ball Movement (23)
    Demonstrating the One Pass We Must Master (24)
    Drills Used in Preparing to Operate the Offense (25)

2. How to Align the Destroyer Offense Against
    Zone Presses 30

    Alignment Against the Mid-Court Zone Press (35)
    Alignment Against Half-Court Zone Presses
       from Base Line (36)
    Using the Offense with Three Left-Handers on
       the Team (38)

3. How to Execute the Destroyer Offense 41

    First Movement of the Offense (44)
    Execution Against the 3–2 Three-Quarter
       Court Zone Press (51)
    Sideline Interchange Drill (51)

4. HOW TO ORGANIZE A COMPLEMENT TO THE DESTROYER
OFFENSE (THE "DESTROYER SET") 56

Alignment of the "Destroyer Set" Offense (59)
Execution of the "Destroyer Set" Offense (59)
Guard Around Series (72)
How to Perfect the "Destroyer Set" (72)
Drills to Implement the "Destroyer Set" (74)
Conversion from the "Destroyer Set" to Defense (79)

Part II
Defensive Complements to the Destroyer

5. HOW DEFENSIVE CHANGES IN THE GAME AFFECT THE
DESTROYER 85

Conversion from Offense to Defense (86)
Systematic Defensive Variation (90)
Fundamental Considerations in Converting
from Offense to Defense (92)

6. HOW TO DEVELOP TOUGH MAN-TO-MAN DEFENSE 94

Defensive Talk (97)
Defensive Shoulder Alignment (98)
Over the Top (99)
Sliding (99)
1–on–1 Drills (100)
2–on–2 Drills (100)
3–on–3 Drills (100)
Defensing the Post (102)
Defensing the Feed Pass (104)
Defensing the Weakside Drive (105)
Weakside Drive Defensive Drill (109)

7. HOW TO GET GOOD USAGE OF ZONE PRESSES 112

Predicting the Score Before the Game Is Played (113)
Trapping in Zone Presses (114)
Relieving Back Line Pressure (119)
The 1–2–2 Zone Press (123)
Shutting Off the Honey (125)

The 2–2–1 Zone Press   (129)
The 1–2–2 Traditional but Trapping Zone   (135)
The One-Half Diamond–Two Defense   (137)
The 3–2 Mid-Court Zone Press   (145)

Part III
Getting Possession and Controlling Tempo in the Destroyer Offense

8. HOW TO DRILL FOR EFFECTIVE REBOUNDING 151

The Rule Innovation for Practice
   and the Big Man   (152)
The Jump Shot   (153)
The Lay-Up   (153)
The One-Hand Push Shot   (154)
Post Man Shooting   (154)
Defensing the Out-of-Bounds Play   (154)
The Trailer Play in the Fast Break   (154)
Team Rebounding   (155)
The Rule Change and Fouling   (155)
A Sequel to the Practice Rule Change   (156)
Defensive Rebounding Drills   (157)
The Defensive Rebounding Drill with Opposition   (159)
The 5–on–5 Rebounding Drill   (159)
The "Tiger Drill" (161)
The Head-to-Head Defensive Rebounding Drill   (162)
Rebounding from the Defensive
   Free Throw Alignment   (164)
Theory and Reality   (165)

9. HOW TO DEVELOP ACCURATE FREE THROW SHOOTING 166

Body Mechanics in Free Throw Shooting   (167)
The Entire Season's Free Throw Shooting Plan   (168)
The Free Throw Practice Timetable   (169)
Hit-the-Rim Drill   (170)
The "I'm Sorry, Coach" Attitude   (171)
Thinking Your Way to Good Free Throw Shooting   (171)
Statistical Analyses of Free Throw Shooting
   and the Schedule   (173)

10. How to Develop Good Ball Movement 175

Pointing (175)
The End-of-Practice Drill (177)
Mass Shuffle Passing Drill (179)
Back-of-the-Hand Passing Drill (180)
Fast Break Passing Drill (181)
The Come-up-at-You Passing Drill (182)
"Rolling Ball" Passing Drills (185)
Lay-Up and Ball Recovery Drill (185)
Five-Man Post Passing Drill (187)
1–on–1, 2–on–2 and 3–on–3 Passing Drills (189)
Figure-Eight Under-the-Basket Passing Drill (190)
The 3–on–2 Fast Break Passing Drill (192)
Sideline Baseball Pass Drill (193)
Jump Ball Situations (193)
The Offensive Jump Ball Plan (195)
The Defensive Jump Ball Plan (198)
The Indefinite Jump Ball Plan (200)
Jump Ball Situations and the Officials (201)
Pre-Practice Drills (202)
Seven Finger Push-Ups (203)
Wall-Leg Exercise (203)
Volleyball Taps (203)
Touching the Rim 30 Times (204)
Reverse Turn Leaps (204)
Jump Rebound Drill (204)
Hop-Skip-Jump Drill (204)
Kangaroo Leap (205)
Individual Ball Handling Drill (205)
Scissors Jump (205)
Theory of Ball Movement (205)

Index 209

KEY TO DIAGRAMS

————————————————▶ *PATH OF PLAYER*

∙∙∙∙∙∙∙∙∙∙∙∙∙∙∙∙∙∙∙∙▶ *PATH OF BALL*

∿∿∿∿∿∿∿∿∿∿∿▶ *DRIBBLE*

↙ *PICK OR SCREEN*

⊘ *POSITION OF BALL*

Basketball's
Destroyer Offense

An Offense for
the Future

1 • • • • • • • • •

How to Put Together the Destroyer Offense

In accordance with the dictate of the National Collegiate Athletic Association, we begin our basketball season on October 15th. All planning for the season has been completed in the summer months, even though we are aware, of course, that many adjustments will have to be made to that planning as the season progresses. And if you should decide to use the subject of this chapter, the Destroyer Offense, I suggest you start to do so on the first day of your season—we do! We feel the offense is a vital part of our program since it neutralizes zone pressure defenses and therefore permits us to use patterned offenses, which we like to do. The offense is simple; so simple that at times it occurs to me not to be an offense at all. For all its simplicity, however, there are two phases of the offense which must be executed perfectly if it is to succeed.

We try to lay down the basis for the offense on the first day of our season. We impress the importance of accurate ball movement on players from that day to the last ball game of the season. I concern myself with that thought 12 months a year. And then we stress the thought that we must strive for that accurate movement, with the ball being thrown quickly. But the quickness sought will be governed by the accuracy achieved. Accurate ball movement is our first goal and to do so quickly is our second.

These two thoughts are essential to successful use of the "Destroyer Offense." We don't use the words naming the offense the first day but talk about accurate and quick ball movement while keeping them in mind. Many other things are covered the first day, but we also leave 15 minutes to describe our feelings about ball movement. And we are very specific about the things we have to say on the subject. I must admit we do not exemplify the democratic process in our practice sessions. Players have opportunities to air their views, but practice time is not one of them. Our practice sessions are geared to a planned timetable and in a dictatorial atmosphere.

Understanding the Background of the Offense

Understanding the background of the offense could actually be helpful in putting the offense together. If you understand how I was prompted to concoct the movement, it may help you implement it.

The offense which we were to call the "Destroyer" was conceived in my mind a few years ago as I watched a National Football League game on television. As I watched sideline pass patterns executed when short yardage was needed in critical situations, I started to speculate about doing something similar in basketball. I reasoned that if the ball was thrown accurately near the sideline, or in out-of-bounds areas, it might create an indefensible situation. You might say, as I did, "But an accurate pass thrown quickly will do the job no matter where it is thrown." However, that isn't true against defenses which employ two men against one, with results being the defense capitalizes on inexperience, lack of emotional control, etc. Nor is it so when those defenses double- and triple-team the ball in zone press tactics—man-to-man, yes; zone press, not necessarily so.

If the zone presses use the boundary markers as additional defensive men, let's go beyond those markers. I then reached the conclusion, "Let them try to defense the out-of-bounds areas." And I got scared, but I kept thinking.

Football uses a zone press when the defense rushes the passer with more than one man. At that time, someone is open in back of the rush in either game. The problem is to find the open man in a relaxed way which enhances execution. Football's screen pass was an answer to those rushes. The "Destroyer Offense" is an answer to basketball's zone presses. *We throw the ball in out-of-bounds areas to beat them.*

After about a month of paper work and three weeks of work on the floor with our freshman team, the offense came to be essentially as it is explained in this book.

One distinct advantage of using the Destroyer Offense is the fact that the sidelines partially orient our players and their movement automatically. It isn't necessary to say, for example, "Go about one step from the free throw line extended." As the movement occurs, players automatically respect the sideline and come to a halt, period. It is that simple. We do describe their positions and movement up and down the floor, but with talk about one dimension of the floor not necessary, we find our work minimized. In addition, effective execution is simple, even if players vary their alignment greatly along the sideline.

Ideas About Ball Movement

The ideas we stress about ball movement are: (1) faster movement will occur if the ball is passed rather than dribbled; (2) to operate one of our basic offenses, we must master the baseball pass (probably right-handed) to perfection; (3) each type of pass we use must be executed with an accuracy which will permit us to run patterned offenses successfully; (4) no player may use any pass he has not worked to perfect; (5) any player may use any pass he has worked to perfect.

It is my opinion that a boy cannot throw the ball accurately if he tries to do so spontaneously—at least not accurately enough statistically to enable us to play our brand of basketball, patterned offenses—nor accurately enough to help us use our Destroyer Offense, which in turn will guarantee us the opportunity to use our offensive patterns. For my purposes, spontaneous accuracy is nonexistent in a statistical sense. Each player must work diligently on the types of passes he is to use.

We pound and pound on the subject of accurate, quick passing. We insist the former must be our first objective rather than the latter. In fact, we strive for passing accuracy prior to shooting accuracy. *I know accurate shooting is an adjunct to accurate passing.* This then is the beginning of our putting together the Destroyer Offense. I have spoken only in general terms so far, but it is vital to do so if I am to lay down a basis of attitude which is necessary for using the ideas I will explain.

Our next step in successive practice sessions is to acquaint our squad with every zone press imaginable. And we concern ourselves with the parts of the floor where these defenses will be most often used. *Then we tell them (every day)* that we shall use an offense which will ruin any zone press. (Although I am beginning to feel we might be able to beat *any* defense with the Destroyer, we are not yet ready to try.) We let the squad know that we shall counteract man presses with other tactics. Again, our intention is to start convincing the squad that the OFFENSE will work successfully against any zone press *WITH EASE*, wherever and whenever zone presses are used. I think as you read the sections of this book dealing with alignment and execution, you will see why it makes no difference what zone press is used or where. Nevertheless, we still go through every possible zone press and areas where they are most often used.

Demonstrating the One Pass We Must Master

On October 15th, I personally demonstrate the one pass we must master. I do so by placing the squad in the middle of the floor in sitting position. Then I go to the sideline with my back to the players. I place my feet along the sideline in a position (foot position is explained later) permitting me to throw a right-handed baseball pass along the sideline. Then I throw the ball up the line to a manager in position to receive the ball while his feet are in bounds but his hands are extended over the sideline. I then ask any player to defense the pass as I throw it several times. *No one has ever touched the ball.* The manager will adjust away from the sideline if the defender tries to take a ball-you-man position. And this is exactly what will happen in game situations, on occasion. *No one has ever touched the ball. This is the basis of our Destroyer Offense.* No one may play defense in an out-of-bounds area. It is illegal. No one enjoys throwing the ball over out-of-bounds areas, but we shall, *after exacting drill* on some very simple parts of the game of basketball.

Drills Used in Preparing to Operate the Offense

The practice time we spend preparing to operate the offense, especially the drills used to attain perfection of the baseball pass, has proven to have great effects on other passes used. It seems players can throw the ball accurately more consistently in any given instance. Consequently, we feel our mechanical errors have diminished since starting to use the offense. And I am convinced our work with the offense has helped us to shoot more accurately. We throw the sideline pass over an out-of-bounds area so that the receiver receives the ball while both feet are in bounds. I don't feel there is any such thing as perfection but *not a single pass has failed to hit its target for us.*

The position of the feet are such that the passer's right foot is closest to the sideline and his left foot opens to the middle of the floor. The receiver's feet are in reverse position; the right foot opens to the middle of the floor and the left foot is next to the sideline. We use no other pass other than the baseball pass to achieve sideline movement of the ball.

Although we move the ball along the sideline with only the baseball pass, our passing drills do include the two-hand over-the-head pass and the two-hand chest pass. For us that is the order of their importance. I feel that the two-hand over-the-head pass is the safest pass in the game, but it is not best suited to do the job we want done in using the Destroyer Offense. I feel a big part of beating zone presses lies in usage of the baseball pass in areas other than sideline areas.

Initially our drills of the baseball pass are executed in the mid-court area. We run them along the mid-court line, with two

lines of players facing one another *about 5 feet apart*. The line in
the middle of the floor is the passing line. The passer has his left
foot *about 1 foot* from the line and his right foot *a few inches*
from it. As already mentioned, the receiver's position is just the
opposite. The drill is depicted in Diagram 1–1. X1, X2, X3, X7,
X8 and X9 all have balls. X1 and X7 pass to X4 and X10, respectively. After those passes, X2, X3, X8 and X9 move up a slot. After
passing, X1 takes X4's spot; X6 moves to the slot left by X3, while
the other group of six players does the same and the drill continues. Each player must assume the correct receiving position
after he passes.

From the first pass thrown and every pass thereafter, we
holler with the force of an elephant trumpeting if the ball is
dropped. We just do not let the ball fall to the floor. *And in game
situations we have never had that baseball pass dropped—never!*

As the first week unfolds, I try to determine when we should
increase the distance between the passing and receiving lanes. I
have found that if our insistence on excellent execution is tough
enough, we are able to increase the distance about six days after
starting the 15-minute passing drill. If the first drill session is held
late in the first week, we try to increase the distance about Wednes-
day of the second week. Increasing distance, of course, will depend on many factors, but in no case have we had to wait more
than six days. When we do increase the distance, it is to throw
the ball from 8 to 10 feet.

We insist the ball be thrown in a clothesline trajectory. We
don't want the ball going toward the receiver's knees or in an arc
which will cause the receiver to stretch upward. We yell, "On a
line, on a line, on a line," in practice. Yes sir, we want every player
to think of himself as a pitcher hitting a catcher's mitt. We want
control, control and control. And I feel it is asking nothing at all.
I refuse to admit there should be a difference in expecting accurate
shooting or accurate passing. One can lead to another. One is the
other. Both are the same.

Often near the end of the second week of such drill the players
are filled with irritated curiosity. The questions are seen if not
heard: "What are we spending so much time on this for? Why is
he so excited if I drop the ball once in awhile? What good will
this be in a ball game? What was he trying to prove by passing

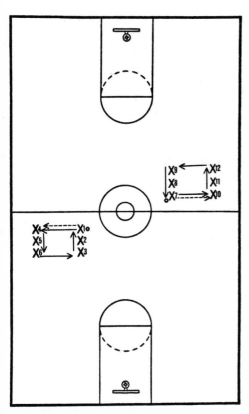

Diagram 1–1.
Mid-court passing drill.

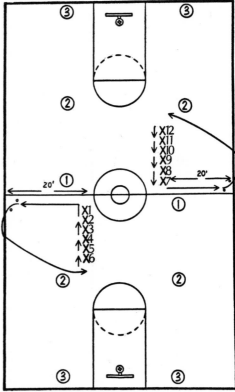

Diagram 1–2.
Sideline receiving drill.

the ball up the sideline?" This is normal and to be expected. Now we add to their wonderment by making them face the sidelines in one line, *about 20 feet from the line,* on each side of the floor. When we holler "Go," a player from each of the two lines sprints to the sideline, making sure to take the correct receiving stance when he gets there. They may not touch the line and no ball is used. This is shown in Diagram 1-2. X1 and X7 sprint to the sideline. They both go to the end of their respective lines as shown. Then each player goes in his turn. We have only one player going on each side at a time which allows us to check his stop and receiving position very carefully. We drill this movement in areas 1, 2 and 3 as Diagram 1-2 shows.

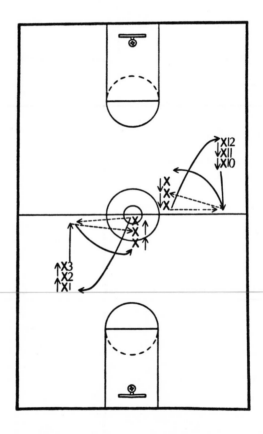

Diagram 1-3. *Mid-court sprint-and-pass drill.*

Early in the third week we go back to the mid-court area and have players in one line sprint to the mid-court line, where they receive a pass from the line in the middle of the floor. This is shown in Diagram 1–3. In passing back to the lines toward the middle of the floor, only a two-hand chest pass is used.

The only reason we run these drills in the middle of the floor is to allow us to see the action better and to keep things moving better than we can along the sideline. And, is it coincidental that the drills are more difficult to watch by a defense when executed along the sideline? I think it is. No one plays defense out of bounds. It's illegal. And it is difficult for even a spectator to watch sideline play, be he a coach, a defensive man or someone up in the stands. Yes, the Destroyer Offense helps to make the defensive man a spectator and not a participant. No one plays offense or defense out of bounds except those using similar movement of the ball, as is done in the Destroyer Offense.

On Monday of the fourth week we explain (diagram and demonstrate) the entire offense, but not any of the variations from the basic offense. After this explanation, we spend 15 minutes daily drilling the plan. In so doing, we use no defenses. It is now opportune for me to explain the Destroyer Offense alignment.

2 • • • • • • • •

How to Align
the Destroyer Offense
Against Zone Presses

The alignment of the Destroyer Offense is basically the same against all zone presses wherever they are used on the floor. We drill movement from alignment in the mid-court area, three-quarter court area and full-court area. We are not really concerned *when* a zone press will be used against us, so we do not run practice drills by setting the stage to simulate a particular time of a ball game. Perhaps this offense is unique to explain, since we must consider "the getting to the alignment" as a part of the alignment.

Diagram 2–1 shows our basic alignment after our opponent has made a field goal or a free throw and goes into a full-court zone press. The reason we align three men in a diagonal line from the corner to the middle of the floor is to prevent the press from becoming too tight. This diagonal line principle is used wherever we align in the offense. It gives us depth up the floor, and if not respected, we are ready to throw the long baseball pass whenever the opportunity occurs. The line also forces a press to position itself wider as well. On certain occasions we have X4 *halfway* between the middle of the floor and the far sideline, which poses no problem of execution if one minor adjustment is made. The adjustment is that X5 must remain deep on the strong side so that the back line of the press must stay honest as far as X4 is concerned. We cannot allow the defense to tighten up from that angle. If X4 is *about 5 feet* from the sideline, X5 *about the same distance* from the base line and the defense doesn't respect the alignment, then the long baseball pass possibility exists up the middle or to the far sideline. At other times, we have moved X5 all the way to the base line just to see what the press would do. In any case we can operate the offense without major adjustments, as you will see. Diagram 2–1 shows that we may move X4 and X5 as indicated, in order to widen and deepen the press without going all the way to the alignment of the men shown in Diagram 2–2.

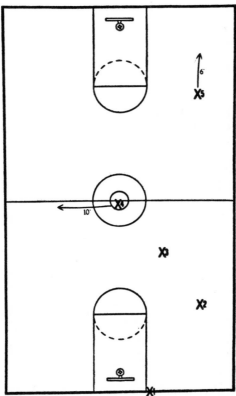

Diagram 2–1. *Basic alignment against full-court zone press after field goal.*

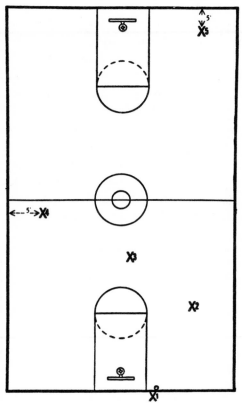

Diagram 2–2. *Deep and wide alignment.*

    In "getting to the alignment" after gaining possession via a turnover, we tell the man gaining possession to dribble the ball to the nearest point on the sideline or the nearest point on the base line, preferably the former. One of the guards is drilled to sprint to the first receiving position *about 8 to 10 feet* from the man with the ball. The other players move to receiving positions in order, just as is the case when the ball is put in play from out of bounds. Diagram 2–3 depicts movement to the sideline in a random turnover situation. Diagram 2–4 shows player and ball movement to the base line when possession is gained on the other side of the floor. Obviously, if we were a left-handed ball club (which I shall talk about later), we would use the left-hand sideline.

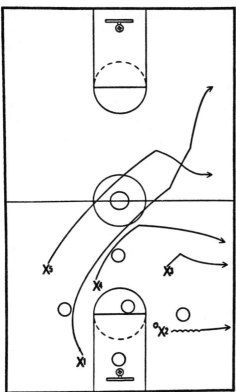

Diagram 2–3.
Random turnover alignment.

Diagram 2–4.
Random turnover alignment.
(Opposite side.)

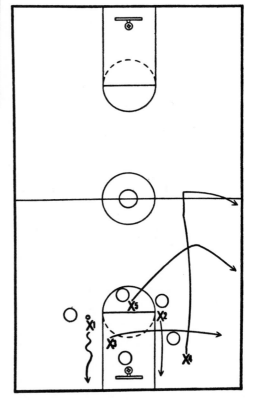

We drill these random situations in our daily 15-minute sessions, which are given over to counteracting zone presses. At times we drill 1-on-1 or 2-on-2 situations, but usually we run the drills with the 5-on-5 arrangement. In the drills we insist that the receivers do not get to the sideline too quickly, which would invite a "ball you man" defensive effort. The defensive man near the action would then have time to get there before the ball does. That is no problem either, however, once we have drilled the entire offense.

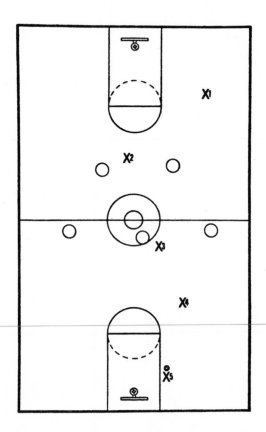

Diagram 2–5. *Alignment against mid-court zone press.*

Alignment Against the Mid-Court Zone Press

If a mid-court zone press is organized, we align as seen in
Diagram 2–5. The mid-court press as well as the three-quarter court
zone press is pleasant to work against. Diagram 2–6 illustrates
alignment against the three-quarter court effort. X5 gains possession and passes to X1. X1 dribbles away from the press to the
sideline. We want to decrease the angle existing between himself

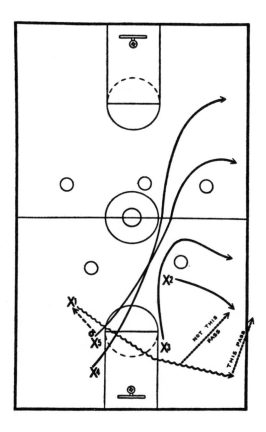

Diagram 2–6. *Alignment against three-quarter court
zone press.*

and the receiver, X2. X2 takes a position a little farther up the floor simply because *we want the defense engaged.* We want our opponents at a distance from which they can try to gain possession, which will result in bypassing their defense along the sideline. Of what value would it be to use alignment or execution if the ball was moved along the sideline and did not bypass them? We want them where we can cause their defense to make an error. X3 is closer to the mid-court line (about 12 feet from it) and X4 will be about 15 feet from the base line in our front court area. X5 may align anywhere in the front court area, as long as he times his move to the sideline so as to be about 15 feet from X3 should the defense cause the offensive movement to progress that far. We want him to be a rover and to call for the long pass if the defense tightens up too much toward the ball.

Alignment Against Half-Court Zone Presses from Base Line

The half-court zone press alignment is shown in Diagram 2–7. This defense minimizes the problem of alignment. We will align the same, but X2 may not have to move toward the sideline to receive the first pass; therefore, we place him more toward the center of the floor. X3 aligns on the mid-court line. X4 is halfway between center court and the basket. X5 plays the rover role and is ready to go to the sideline if defensive pressure is applied from center court forward. If there is no defensive pressure X5 will align on the weak side, which should force the defense to respect a bigger man that close to "home plate."

As might be expected, we have found best results are achieved with our best ball handling guard and best moving guard in the X1 slot. This is true against any zone press thrown at us anywhere on the floor. We want the bigger men receiving the ball and, after bypassing the press, to be in positions of penetration which will be an assist to implementation of our patterned offenses.

If there is one left-hander on the club, we place him in the X3 or X4 position. If both guards are left-handers, we will take the ball up the left sideline. Of course, we would have to run drills accordingly. We have not had two left-handed guards since we started using the offense. If we were to use the left sideline, the

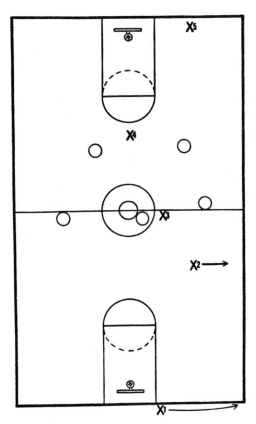

Diagram 2–7.
Alignment against half-court zone press from base line.

Diagram 2–8.
Left sideline alignment.

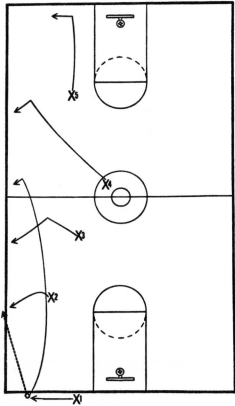

alignment would be the same on the other side of the floor as seen in Diagram 2–8.

X1, after making the first pass, would fill the sideline spot in the area of X4 and the latter would move as shown. X5 would be forced to a deep post position and be ready to take the sideline position as well. Although we have never used the left sideline in running the offense, I know most zone presses are demoralized after the first two sideline passes are thrown. This is true because we find ourselves with possession in the mid-court area, despite the oppositions' pressing tactics. X3 would be limited to one particular pass, that being the two-hand over-the-head pass. The ball would be thrown at a slight angle to the sideline rather than in a straight line over the out-of-bounds area.

X2 is normally our second guard. There are times, however, when either X3, X4 or X5 will be in the third-, fourth- or fifth-man spots. We drill accordingly, with these players filling any of those positions. We tell them to fill the gap closest to them and gear their movement to actual reception of the ball by the man before them.

On one occasion against a mid-court press, our ball club took the ball around the corner (without ever having drilled the movement) and the man in the X5 slot went to the base line, took the last pass, pivoted to a position about 4 feet from the basket and hit the shot in a 1-on-1 situation. That's what we like to see—the situation graduated down to a 1-on-1 situation and bypassing would-be "traps." Where is the zone press at such times? The best pressure it can exert will be of a man-to-man variety. I don't care what zone press starts against us.

Using the Offense with Three Left-Handers on the Team

Obviously, if we had three left-handers on our team, we would align on the left side of the floor. As mentioned, we have never encountered that situation. In such case, however, we would drill the offense on both sides of the floor and use the X1 and X5 positions for the right-handers. We would do so without regard for height or ball handling ability. X2, X3 and X4 would be limited to use of the over-the-head pass on the right side of the floor. Being a left-handed unit, so called, would cause me to place more importance on that happenstance than would alignment based on height or maneuvering ability.

It is true we have had no experience in which our opponent has started a ball game with a pressing zone in, and only in, our offensive area. If we were met with such a situation, we would still align on the sideline, invite the traps, execute the sideline ball movement pattern and go right around the corner of the floor. Diagram 2–9 indicates that alignment.

I feel, as I write this, that the alignment of the Destroyer Offense is so simple it is too elementary to be worthy of writing about. Anyone writing a book about offensive basketball ought to have more to say about alignment. But our experience with this offense dispels any qualms I might have about brevity. We have

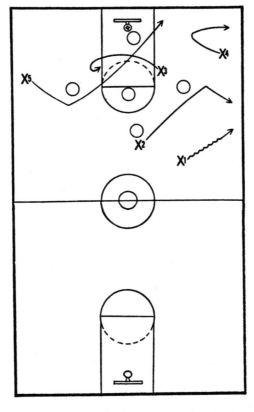

Diagram 2–9. *Around the corner against pressure zone.*

used it against many different zone presses. The results we have enjoyed have caused me to think, "Gee, is this a case which exemplifies the thought—effective things are often the most simple things?" Perhaps so.

3 • • • • • • • • •

How to Execute
the Destroyer Offense

I feel I would be remiss if I were to explain the execution of the offense without first talking about the mental attitude it helps build. I hope you have noticed one thing—we do not talk about the mental attitudes we will have to maintain in operating against zone presses. We do not use such terminology as "don't get excited," "take your time," "relax," "forget the pressure," etc. We don't talk that way because I don't feel such talk achieves very much. We do tell our players, show them and drill them in the use of the Destroyer Offense. This offense will contribute greatly in building those attitudes necessary to beat zone presses and probably many other well-planned defensive measures. We don't talk about it, the offense does it. Frankly, we have found our squads to be skeptical when we first tell them about this offense. They harbor a natural dislike for throwing the ball over out-of-bounds areas. But when I ask them, "What if I tell you no zone press will ever bother you again, and all we have to do is sprint a short distance, stop correctly and throw one type of pass accurately—what would you think then? Is it too much to ask you to be an accurate passer—just as accurate as the good passing quarterback in football must be? Is it too much to ask that you throw one pass that must never fail?" Some of the skepticism then

begins to disappear. Later this is followed by a reaction of wonderment on their part. *But after the first pass in a game is thrown
successfully, the team's mental attitude becomes something to
warm your heart. Just imagine sitting on the bench free from
worry about zone presses forever.*

I will describe only one game situation in this book which will
attest to the soundness of the offense (although many more occurred).

In a recent season, we played host to a strong Rhode Island
College club. They came at us with a starting five of superior
height and good speed at the guard positions. Our biggest boy
was 6 feet, 2 inches. Without the "Destroyer," it would have been
an embarrassing evening. Our game plan included use of the
"Double Offense" or "Destroyer Set" and great care to take only
the percentage shot. The first half was a low-scoring affair. In the
second half, Rhode Island went into a mid-court zone press in an
effort to speed up the tempo. Twice we bypassed their press with
the Destroyer and went into the Double Offense. And it took us
one pass each time to get by their zone press. The offense made it
possible for us to play our kind of ball game, despite a lack of
height, speed or great talent. It allowed us to control the tempo
with our offensive play, and what a job it has always been to
control tempo with defensive play—that's one of the reasons zone
presses were born. Now we are able to go toward an offensive-
defensive balance again, since we can deny tempo determination to
zone pressing teams. We lost the Rhode Island ball game by five
points in the final seconds, but we would not have belonged on
the same floor with them if we could not have used the Destroyer.

Rule #7, Section #6, (b) states:

> Until the passed ball has crossed the plane of the bound-
> ary line, no player shall have any part of his person over
> the boundary line.

For this reason, our first pass is made to a receiver who com-
plies with the rule cited. We do so extend players' arms over the
boundary line with successive passes.

With this as background, it is a pleasure to try to explain the
execution of the Destroyer Offense.

We believe in moving toward the ball when trying to receive

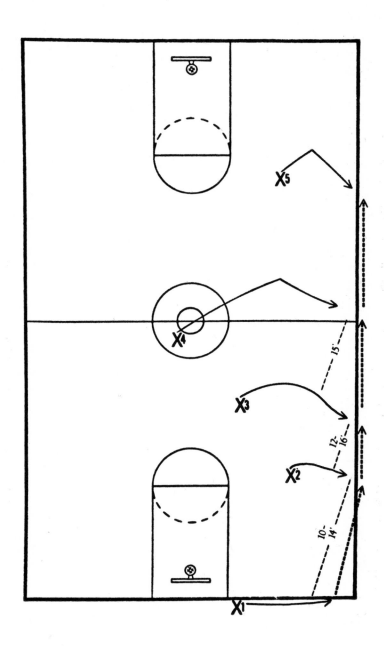

Diagram 3–1. *Basic movement.*

it. We comply with this belief in the Destroyer as we do in all our offenses. This dictates that initial movement from alignment must be slightly away from the ball and then back to it. I think all of the diagrams will show that, but if not, please be aware that such should be the case.

First Movement of the Offense

Diagram 3–1 illustrates the first movement in the offense. X1 moves as shown. X2 holds a long second and then moves to the sideline. X1 throws the baseball pass in a flight path which cuts the corner of the base line in accordance with the pertinent rule cited. As X1 delivers the pass, X3 moves quickly to the sideline. X2 turns and throws the baseball pass into the backboard hand of X3. As X2 delivers the pass, X4 takes the sideline position and receives the ball while in the stance described earlier in this part of the book.

Yes, X1 throws the ball from out of bounds so that it is received by an in-bounds player making reception over an out-of-bounds area. The receiver has both feet in bounds, which makes interpretation of the ball location as in bounds. As the ball moves up the floor it remains in bounds for the same reason, although the flight of the ball is over out-of-bounds territory. No defense can be practiced, spontaneously carried out or even thought about in efforts to counteract such ball movement. This is the basis for the entire offense; the rules prohibit defensive play to be executed in an out-of-bounds area. The defense may, of course, duplicate the offensive maneuvering, which would be to position itself along the sideline and use the arms over the out-of-bounds area.

We drill the basic offensive movement as shown in Diagram 3–2. We have three men in each of the X1, X2, X3, X4 and X5 lines. Guards are in the X1 and X2 lines as the drill starts. After X1 passes to X2 (as shown, about 10 to 14 feet), he goes to the rear of the X2 line. X2 becomes the last man in the X3 line after passing to X3 (about 12 to 16 feet). The movement continues this way in each line. The pass from X3 to X4 covers from 14 to 18 feet, and X4 will pass to X5 from 15 to 20 feet. The distances of the passes increase a bit as we go up the floor since we are, at this point, theoretically leaving behind some of the defensive people.

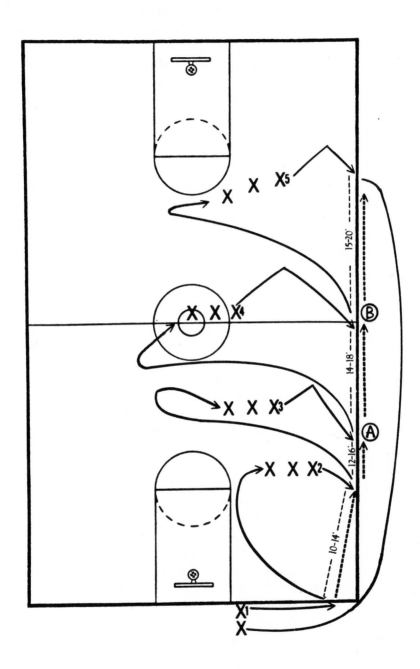

Diagram 3–2. *Drill of basic offense.*

But the distances of these passes will have to be regulated according to the defensive effort and the passing ability developed. X5, after receiving the ball, dribbles it around the outside of the floor to the X1 line. When the drill starts, the second man in the X1 line also has a ball. Then we supply balls as needed to keep balls and people on the move. Coaches stand at positions A and B.

Although we want the guards running the X1 and X2 positions during actual competition, we also desire every player to be experienced in every position. This prepares us for those zone presses in which bigger men are used deep in our back court.

In the event you are now disgusted, let me tell you that the only defensive action we have experienced, which had any effect at all, was when a defensive man knifed between the passer and the would-be receiver. This has happened after the defense had seen the movement once or twice. The result of such effort was that they knocked the ball out of bounds (still our ball) or they went out of bounds with the ball (same result). In another defensive effort, the defense went in the air over the sideline, turned and threw the ball back. Since our alignment is made to move to the sideline, we came up with the ball and went toward the basket, with the advantage of one man over the defense. *We have never lost possession because of sideline defensive efforts.*

Diagram 3–3 shows the movement of each player after each pass is thrown. I assume in the diagram that the ball is moved to the other end of the floor and toward the basket. The diagram is without any deviation which could be caused by defensive errors along the way.

Following the first pass, X1 moves away from the action on the ball if he is certain trapping is not imminent on X2. At the head of the circle, he must decide if trapping is being applied or not. If X2 is under no stress, he continues as shown. This movement should make the press stay in a partially "stretched" alignment. And, of course, it does counteract defensive pressure in a small area. X2 must be aware of X3's situation as the former moves away from the action. X1 keys his continued movement down the floor on the second X3 has possession. X4 reacts similarly to X2, but we want him to hold his position in the center floor area since he may be the next receiver on the sideline. If X3 does pass to X4 on the sideline, he then goes to the top of the free throw

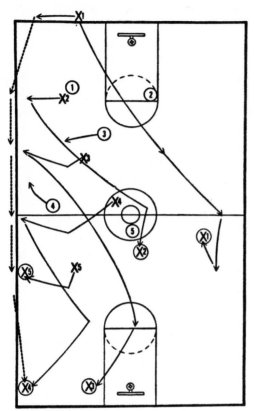

Diagram 3–3.
*Complete offense without
variation.*

Diagram 3–4.
*From the "Destroyer" Offense
into the Double alignment.*

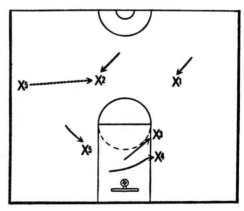

circle. X4 passes to X5 and goes to the free throw line extended. If pressure is still applied, X4 will go to the base line and take the pass which will cut the corner from X5. If execution reaches this point, X3 must go to the base line also and he will try to score.

If defensive efforts are relaxed when X5 receives the ball, he will look for the guard, X2, and if X2 has possession, we are ready to run one of our patterned offenses. X1 would move into the other guard slot while X5 moves into the post area. This would give us the basic alignment of the Double Offense. Since we align in the Double Offense before going to any of our other patterned offenses, either against man-to-man or zone defenses, we are also ready to use any of our patterns. If X2 has possession, the other four men move into the Double alignment as seen in Diagram 3–4.

We don't want X2 to bring the ball up the floor even one step, since he would probably head into zone press tactics. We do want him to go toward the sideline, moving slightly away from X1. If the defense goes with X2's movement, X2 must return toward the middle of the floor when he catches O1's weight going the wrong way. It is inevitable that the defense will try to get into what is really a ball-you-man alignment. We insist, therefore, that X2 always take at least two of his sprint steps toward the sideline. It is difficult to get the defense to commit with any less distance. Catching O1 going the wrong way, X2 comes back. That movement is shown in Diagram 3–5. X2's return movement should be in an arc slightly away from X1. If X1 releases to X2, X1 goes to the sideline position which would have been taken by X2. X2 then dribbles in an arc away from X1 (toward the sideline) and passes to X1 in the sideline position. Only once have we had the second defensive man beat our receiver to the sideline. In such case, X2 executes the same interchange with X3.

X3, X4 and X5 merely hold their positions. But if the defensive men in areas near them move to apply pressure, they are drilled to move as the situation is shown in Diagram 3–6a. In this case, X4 moves closer to the ball, which makes ball movement on the sideline from X1 to X2, back to X1 and then to X4. X3 serves as an outlet if needed. If X3 does get the ball, he dribbles to the same sideline and we go up the line. Diagram 3–6b shows the plan for the drill of sideline pressure.

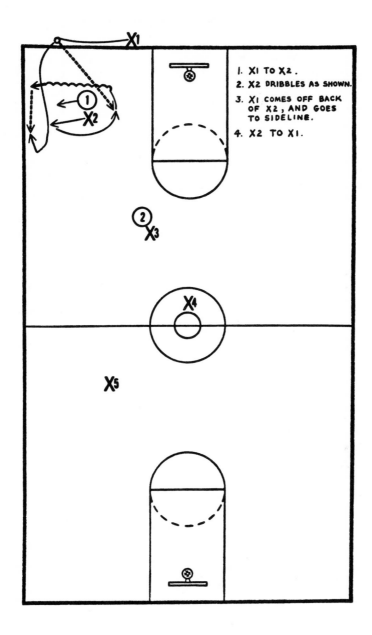

1. X1 TO X2.
2. X2 DRIBBLES AS SHOWN.
3. X1 COMES OFF BACK OF X2, AND GOES TO SIDELINE.
4. X2 TO X1.

Diagram 3–5. *Sideline interchange.*

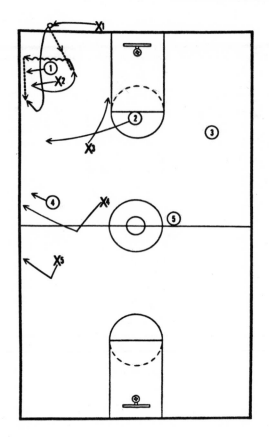

Diagram 3–6a. *Reaction to sideline pressure.*

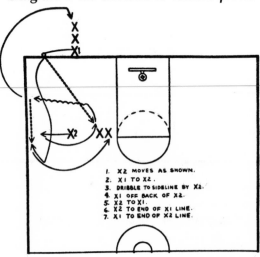

1. X2 MOVES AS SHOWN.
2. X1 TO X2.
3. DRIBBLE TO SIDELINE BY X2.
4. X1 OFF BACK OF X2.
5. X2 TO X1.
6. X2 TO END OF X1 LINE.
7. X1 TO END OF X2 LINE.

Diagram 3–6b. *Drill plan for sideline pressure.*

Execution Against the 3-2 Three-Quarter Court Zone Press

This defensive effort would result in a 3-on-3 situation in the area of the ball, while X3 and X5 would be serious threats for outlet passes. The 3-2 three-quarter court press shown in Diagram 3–8 (page 54) illustrates the situation. O4 would have to be interested in X4 and O3 involved with X3 (from a rear position), and O5 is halfway between someone and no one. X5 is a two-point threat under such conditions. It seems to me the defense would be foolish to adjust in that way. And I don't think the opposition is ever foolish . . . at least I don't plan on it.

Sideline Interchange Drill

The movement demands a page to explain, but in action we just holler "break back" if the defense adjusts as described. If the defense is in a two-man front, we react the same way. A 1-on-1 alignment must develop unless the defense brings defensive pressure from the weak side, in which case X4 or X5, or both, move to the weakside alignment. At that point, there is a good chance the weak side will become the strong side in a hurry. X5's role as a rover meets any defensive adjustment in their back line. But let's face it, we are able to force 1-on-1 coverage and execute penetration up the floor because of the out-of-bounds pass they cannot defense. The basic offensive principle of the plan is indefensible.

I feel the "break back" part of the offense places the defense in an impossible situation. They are on the ropes and all we have to do is use their own defensive momentum to cause the downfall of the pressure. If a similar defensive adjustment hits us farther up the floor than that outlined, we react in the same way but with one other adjustment. Again that adjustment is shown in Diagram 3–8. We run the drill with 12 ball players since any more has seemed to make it cumbersome.

We are not really concerned about using the Destroyer Offense, however, after the third or fourth pass. It has been our experience that most zone presses get out of the press if we "bypass" their defense with three or four passes. Such being the case, we are then able to move to one of our patterned offenses. In fact, most presses abandon their plan if one or two passes "bypass" them.

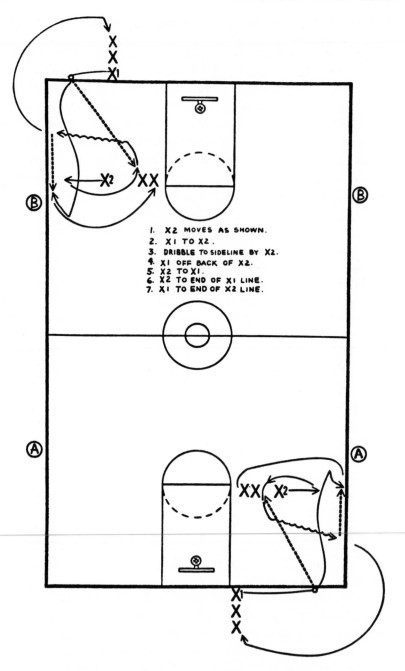

1. X2 MOVES AS SHOWN.
2. X1 TO X2.
3. DRIBBLE TO SIDELINE BY X2.
4. X1 OFF BACK OF X2.
5. X2 TO X1.
6. X2 TO END OF X1 LINE.
7. X1 TO END OF X2 LINE.

Diagram 3–7. *Drill for sideline interchange.*

The X1 line moves as shown (Diagram 3–7); X1 passes to X2 as the latter breaks back in reaction to the aggressive defensive movement toward the sideline. X1 goes up the sideline and takes the receiving position, which would have been taken by X2 if there had been no defensive movement to the sideline. X2 dribbles to the sideline after X1 clears, and then he passes over the out-of-bounds area to X1. If the defensive pressure to the sideline continues on X1, he will break back and the same interchange occurs again.

We have found it necessary to run the "break back" drill in the mid-court and three-quarter court areas. For some zany reason, people become confused when running the movement in areas where it has not been drilled. This is especially true if the drill is not run on both ends of the floor. We have also found it to be more effective if we drill the movement by doing so with just two men. We do not, however, execute the drill all the way up the floor without stopping. This being the case, we drill the interchange from standstill positions in areas A and B. In Diagram 3–8 we anticipate defensive pressure, with or without traps. We assume pressure can only be exerted along the sideline.

Assuming X2 has possession, we are in a trap situation if O1 and O2 decide to converge on the ball. X1 must check O1's reaction; if he goes toward the ball even one step, X1 breaks hard toward the middle of the floor. X3 goes to the sideline. X1 must look into the ball, and he hollers "me" if the trap is imminent. Now X2 can release to X3 or X1. (We allow no other word than "me" to be used in this situation.) If the pass goes to X3, he will try to pass the ball to X5. In any case, X1, X3, X4 and X5 give us an advantage of one man in a fast break situation. It would seem impossible that any zone press would operate with a four-man back line alignment. At least I have never seen such zone press alignment. If it is used, it would mean that zone pressing would be impossible in our back court area.

This explains the entire offense and the drills we use to try to perfect it. If you try it, I am sure you will find occasions when your opponent will abandon the press after you bypass his best efforts with your first pass. There will be other occasions when your opponent will be a team which spends a lot of time using zone presses, but knowing of your intended retaliation to its

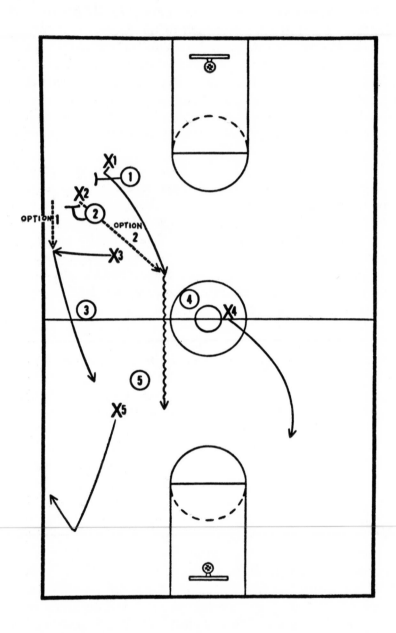

Diagram 3–8. *Adjustment to continued pressure "up the line."*

efforts, it will not even try in your ball game with it. And very possibly the offense, the entire offense, may not be explained because it will be a rare case indeed when you will need it in its entirety. The Destroyer acts upon zone presses seeking to demoralize you offensively; in a way it causes demoralization of the would-be demoralizers. And if they place great importance on their zone presses, you may find them to be even less than a mediocre ball club. They face a result of panic because:

(1) Playing defense along the sideline with ball-you-man efforts really chases the defense into patterns they have not drilled. (You are chasing them and they aren't chasing you.) When that happens, they prefer to use defenses they have drilled. And if they drill ball-you-man defense, they have forgotten their zone tactics by definition.

(2) As I think you will agree, minimal variations are necessary to execute the basic movement against defensive adjustments. And the ball can be taken to the sideline for safe passing if you want to get out of the variation at any time.

(3) For all practical purposes, passing drills are concentrated on only two types of passes.

(4) Speed, height or any other physical attributes of your opposition are neutralized.

Finally, we are aware that the Destroyer Offense might be used effectively against man-to-man pressing defenses, but one consideration makes me hesitate to try it. I would not like to see the ball taken to the sideline in pell-mell fashion. If one man plays just one man, consideration of ball position by the defense, in a team sense, is of secondary importance. This fact might, I think, allow the defense to chase us to the sideline in pell-mell fashion. I cannot accept that type of play in efforts to combat pressure defenses of whatever kind. But I might add that we are toying with a few thoughts which might help us use the Destroyer against any press, zone or man-to-man.

4 • • • • • • • • •

How to Organize a Complement to the Destroyer Offense (The "Destroyer Set")

In my first season at Plymouth State, I inherited a starting five consisting of player heights of two boys at 6 feet even, two boys at 6 feet, 2 inches and one boy at 6 feet, 3 inches. Although my knowledge of our league was superficial, and although it was a small college conference, I assumed this would not be enough size to make our team a contender for the conference crown. In September, therefore, I decided to try to use at least one offense which would place three of our players on the offensive boards. Even if it wouldn't give us a second effort to score from missed shots, it would at least enable us to combat the fast-breaking ball clubs in the way I thought it should be done, in the offensive board area. The result of the paper work in September and October of that year evolved into what we now call our "Destroyer Set." Initially the offense was a double post or triple post affair, but later it developed into a lane-stack offense. I believe it makes sense to visualize it and consider it as a supplement to the "Destroyer Offense." Therefore, I have dubbed it the "Destroyer Set."

We lost our opening game on our floor that first season to a good Salem State College ball club by 26 points. In March we played the same team on their floor for the Conference Championship, and lost by 5 points in a ding-dong battle. I am convinced the progress we evidently made was due in great part to the use of the "Destroyer Set." We reached that championship ball game in a conference consisting of 17 state colleges in the six New England states.

Since that first year we have changed and added, but never deleted, any of the offensive thrusts which were used in the original version. Many high schools in New Hampshire and Vermont now use this offense in near duplication of the State College version. Coach Bob Tipson of Champlain Junior College uses the basic offense, with a few new wrinkles, which I think makes a very effective offense. Coach Carl McAllister of Fall Mountain High School and Coach Jim Krug of Plymouth High School have enjoyed much success with their versions of the "Double" or "Destroyer Set." I think it is fair to assume there are other ex-Plymouth players using the offense in their coaching efforts, and with success—at least I have never seen the offense used to the dissatisfaction of the coach involved.

How can the "Destroyer Set" or "Double" offense help you? There is no doubt in my mind your team would benefit in the phases of the game I have listed below; I have no doubts because the items mentioned have been tested over a five-year period by college and high school teams, although I cannot attest to any specific number. And perhaps the last statement is unnecessary, since I am convinced the offense will sell itself, when and if it is scrutinized by the many fine high school and college coaches in our country. At the same time I realize, of course, that it will not appeal to every coach, since there are those who do not subscribe to use of patterned offenses.

(1) The offense provides protection for every pass thrown.

(2) Offensive rebounding is strengthened immeasurably.

(3) 1-on-1 play by either guards or post men can be executed easily.

(4) High and low post play are potent parts of the attack.

(5) It is impossible to jam the middle when you want it open.

(6) If you follow our conversion from offense to defense, it can combat the fast-breaking ball clubs where it should be done, before the break can organize.

(7) It is potent against teams with greater height.

(8) It offers opportunities for your opponents to play defense more cautiously or to do so in more of a fouling atmosphere. (We think the offense is one way we have been able to get into the bonus free throw situation early in many ball games.)

(9) Alterations of the offense are simple to fit to your personnel and ideas.

I must add at this point that I believe basketball is a three-man game offensively. The problems existing in the operation of any offense are based on the unoccupied offensive men, or per-haps more correctly put—How can we keep the other two defen-sive men engaged? This is assuming, of course, the defense is of the man-to-man variety. We believe this thought is what is being said when coaches insist their players play well "away from the ball." Success of the "Double," or any other patterned offense, must hinge upon denying the defense the double-team or "trap"; therefore, whatever success is to be realized from the usage of the offense explained in this chapter must be preceded by an ability to beat pressing defenses. And if we cannot do this, then we cannot play patterned ball. Primarily zone presses must be neutralized. We feel we can handle the man-to-man presses without too much trouble. Quite frankly, we seek to recruit the small guard or de-velop one, if we can't recruit him, who has the ability to play successfully in 1-on-1 basketball. We then try to combat the man-to-man presses with his or their play, if we have two of them. If we are successful with such plans, the only threat posed to usage of patterned offenses (including the "Destroyer Set") are the zone presses. And again, quite frankly, they gave us trouble until we inaugurated the "Destroyer." Since that time we have been able to play patterned ball without interruption.

We start from the basic premise that a good offensive man will beat a good defensive man because he knows where he is going and when he is going there. Putting it another way, the defensive man must *react;* whereas, the offensive man *acts.* Remember, we have neutralized the pressing defenses. We insist the offense can determine the tempo if zone presses can be defeated. If the man, playing a man-to-man defense, with his back to the basket, takes a pressing step forward, we feel we can beat him. We want that defensive man up tight *so that his first step must be a backward one.* Such a premise deals with the ball-you-man defenses effectively. We build all our patterned offenses on that one statement. All our practices include defensive practices which are very aggressive. We feel that good defensive play builds our offenses. Offensively, players will develop commensurately with the level of defensive play. So, once we were able to stop worrying about zone presses and ball-you-man defenses, we were able to concentrate on the refinement of our patterned offenses.

Alignment of the "Destroyer Set" Offense

Diagram 4–1 indicates the basic alignment of this offense. As already mentioned I am aware you might argue that it should be called a lane-stack offense, but I see no need to waste time in such discussion. Whatever we call it is of little consequence if it will do the job for both of us.

We would like X5 to be our tallest player. X3, in our league, can operate in his position quite effectively at 6 feet, 2 inches, but he must be capable of quick starts and possess good "chess sense" close to the basket. One of our guards must be able to take the ball to the basket. We will try at times to isolate either a post man or a guard, or both at the same time. That is why we must have at least one guard who can give us the outside threat. And now you might say, "Sure, anyone can win with any offense, if he has the talent." I agree with that statement, but notice I have placed talent requirements on only three players. If you don't have talent in at least three positions, you aren't going to win anyway because of or despite whatever offense you use.

Execution of the "Destroyer Set" Offense

Diagram 4–2 depicts our first movement. I first saw this

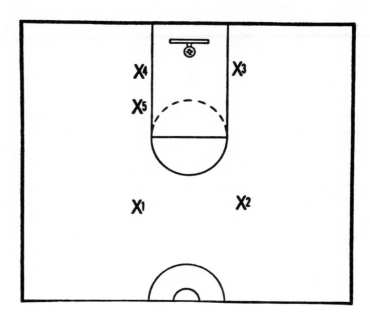

Diagram 4-1.

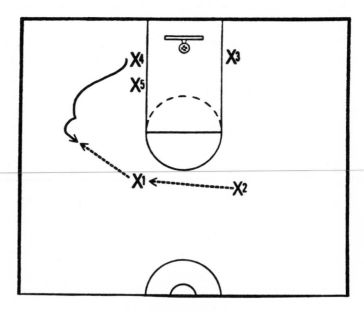

Diagram 4-2.

executed by Coach Ted Owen's University of Kansas team in a Kansas–St. John University ball game. The big Kansas center got 10 of the first 12 points of the ball game while using just this option.

X4 steps out two to four steps (long, quick steps) to accept the pass from X1. We insist that X1 deliver the pass from a dribble toward X4. If the defense pressures him hard, we simply tell him to move so that he is dribbling slightly away from the basket. When X4 receives the ball, we want him to dribble once or twice so he can see, as we call it, "around the corner." We want the four other players to be in passing lanes. In order for that to be possible, we must continue movement as shown while the ball moves from X1 to X4. Diagram 4–3 depicts that movement. In Diagram 4–3 X3 has taken two steps forward, which permits X1 to flatten his drive around him. X2 has faked a move to the weak side and then made himself available to X4 as indicated. X5 remains steadfast. As X1 moves through the lane area, he is in ball reception position with regard to X4; X2 exists as the receiver of the certain

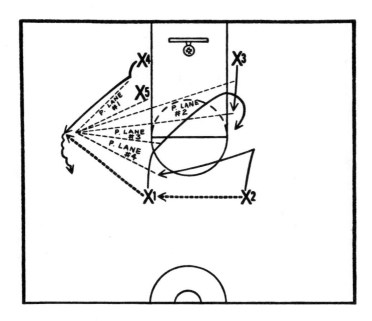

Diagram 4–3.

outlet pass if it is needed; X3 is in a good passing lane before and after X1 clears; the best passing lane of all exists for X5. (Passing lanes are shown by the darkened lines.)

We want to be expedient. We want to score quickly. We always try to move the ball to X5. In order to avail ourselves of all possibilities, we insist that X4 end his dribble so that he is facing the basket.

In Diagram 4–4 I have shown the ball being moved to X5, and we would like that pass *to be an over-the-head two-handed pass.* X5 steps toward the passer and at that point checks to see what his defensive man does. If the defense is honest, he accepts the pass; if the defense is trying to front the situation, X5 must break to the basket. If X5 receives the ball without breaking to the basket, X4 will step in tight, on the basket side, which permits us to execute the "pick and roll" play as seen in Diagram 4–5.

We want X5 to take the shot as soon as possible after he clears the screen. We will take the short jumper in preference to the drive to the basket, although we did have one boy who was able

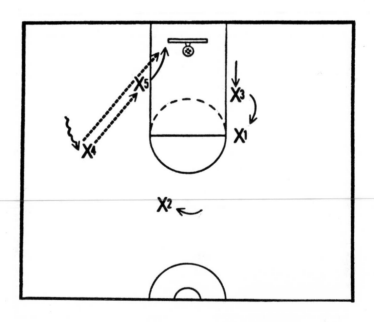

Diagram 4–4.

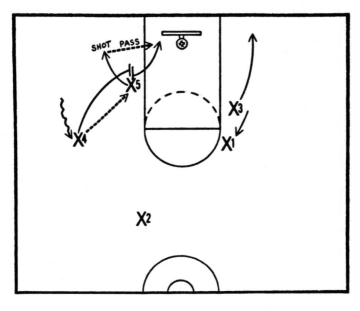

Diagram 4-5.

to execute the latter exceedingly well. Jim Durkee was a 6-foot, 2-inch post man with tremendous leaping power; he scored many points by driving to the basket with this option. Ordinarily, however, we like to take the shot as quickly as possible for two reasons: (1) we feel that if our post men can't hit that 6-foot shot, we will not be using the option anyway; (2) we don't want the defense to have time to recover. X4 rolls with the movement as indicated, and he must move in an inside arc which will open him to the ball better than would an outside arc. Of course the possible switch by the defense is countered by the inside arc movement and the ensuing inside-hand bounce pass. Seeing the screen being set by X4, X3 moves from the weak side to assume rebounding position on that side. He does so from a low post position which he took when the ball was passed to X5. If his man sloughs, X3 must get involved by shouting for the ball.

Diagram 4-6 depicts movement of the ball from X4 to X2 rather than attempting the pick-and-roll play. The pass from X4 to X2 keys continuance of the offense. X1 moves as indicated. X2 passes the ball to X1, and X3 starts toward the middle of the

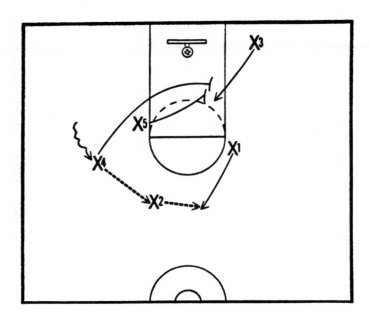

Diagram 4–6.

foul lane as if the action may erupt there—in fact it will, if there
is a decided mis-match at that point. Meanwhile X4 and X5 move
to provide a double screen for X3. We prefer X3 to come over the
top of the screen, but we do not insist that he be limited to such
movement. From experience we have found, however, that the
man playing X3 oftentimes commits a foul as he goes with X3 over
the top. X4 and X5 must be immobile before contact is made.

In Diagram 4–7, X2, after his pass, fake drives to the weak
side, returns and is given the ball by X1. X2 can now move the
ball in a cleared-out area on the weak side for the shot. X2 becomes
the half man in the rebound situation, and X4 gets in rebound
position while X5 will be the middle rebounder. X1 assumes the
safety man role. May I say that we have used the low post penetration off a double screen repeatedly against defenses as aware of
our intentions as our own ball club, with success?

If the defense prevents us from executing the pick-and-roll or
low post option, or any of the possible sloughs are not used advan-
tageously, then we continue as shown in Diagram 4–8. Continuous
action is shown from Diagram 4–6 to Diagram 4–8.

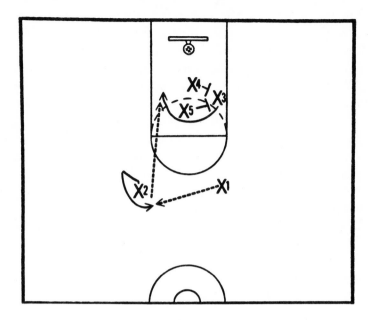

Diagram 4–7.

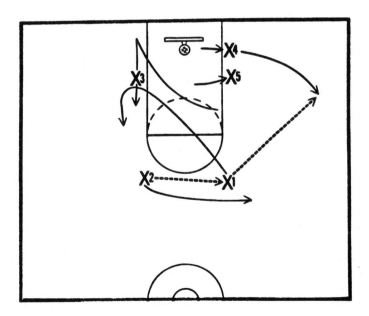

Diagram 4–8.

The movement by X3, X4 and X5 is shown in Diagram 4–8. Now the alignment has moved to the other side of the floor and the offense can be continued.

On occasion the opposition has tried to pressure the step-out pass. When it was first tried it was moderately successful. Successful in the sense that it made entry into the offense somewhat clumsy. It did not cause us to lose possession. When we reminded our players that any one of the three post men could move out to receive the pass, the problem was solved. At times either of the strong-side post men step out, and at other times the weakside man moves all the way over in an interchange with X4. Diagrams 4–9 and 4–10 show that movement.

In Diagram 4–9, X4 fakes the step-out while X5 executes the actual movement. In Diagram 4–10 both X4 and X5 fake the step-out, in turn, and then X3 comes to the strong side while X4 becomes the swing man.

Diagram 4–11 indicates the way we use screening efforts to

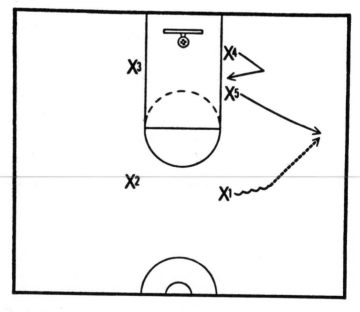

Diagram 4–9.

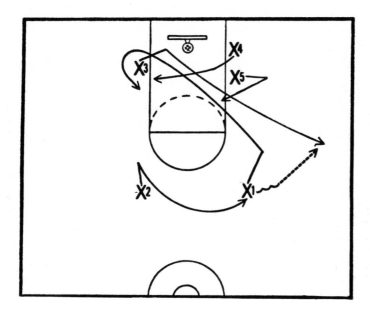

Diagram 4–10.

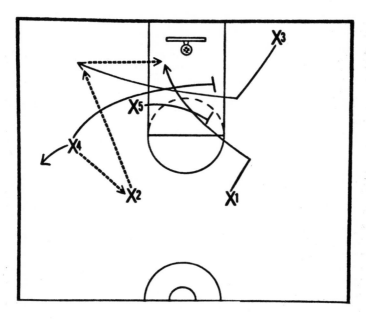

Diagram 4–11.

give the attack potency from the front line. The sequence of movement can be followed by returning to Diagram 4–6, at which time the double screen is being used by X3 to receive the feed pass from X2. The very simple change is that instead of screening for X3, X5 sets a single screen for X1, who has received the ball from X2. X1 returns the ball, fake drives to the weak side and looks to get the ball from X3, who has received it from X2. This is operating a drive series in a cleared-out area.

Diagrams 4–12 through 4–14a and 4–14b indicate the way we isolate in order to play 1-on-1 basketball with any post man or either guard. Such type of play does not detract from the fluidity of the "Destroyer Set." It has proven to be a simple and effective variation. It seems obvious that we can move the basketball to any man in an isolation situation. In a recent season, our great guard and play maker, Jim Lincoln, won at least three ball games with crucial plays down the middle. This tactic was especially successful against Keene State in which game Jim scored seven times down the middle, and three of them brought the 3-point play. Keene tried to play Jim straight away without sloughing, and they were penalized heavily for it. Of course any player assuming a corner position must be ready to move out in any slough situation, and we want him to try to score. In the corner game situation, we have the guard who is not making the play assume the safety man slot in the event of any shot. X3 must go to the rebound position on the right side while X4 and X5 fill the middle and left side, respectively. Diagram 4–14b indicates that movement.

Diagram 4–15 demonstrates the effort involved in taking advantage of shooting opportunities by a good-shooting post man playing the X4 position. Our experience has been that the man in this position can take advantage of many shooting opportunities in the free throw line area. Most recently we used 6-foot, 6-inch Bob Russell in this slot. Bob was not a fast-moving player, but he was quick and he was as good a shooter as we have had since I have been at Plymouth State. In one ball game against Gorham State of Gorham, Maine, he hit 17 out of 19 shots from the field, and all of them were shots coming from the movement explained in Diagram 4–15. Bob ranked high in the national ranking of the NCAA small college division for field-goal shooting

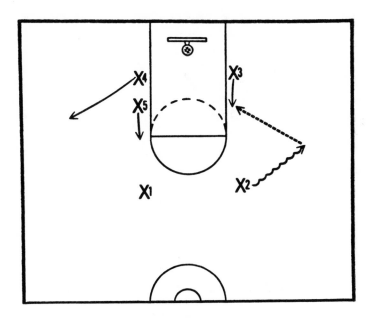

Diagram 4–12.

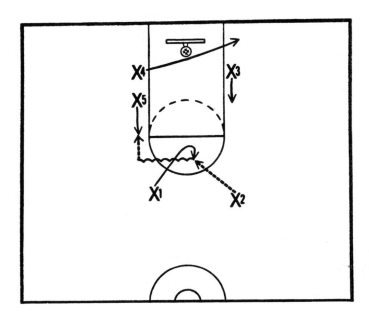

Diagram 4–13.

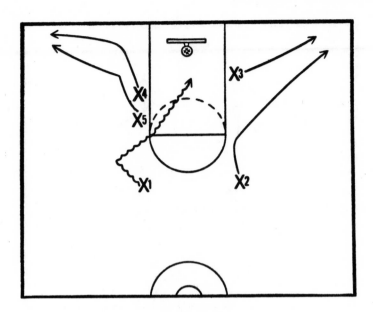

Diagram 4–14a.

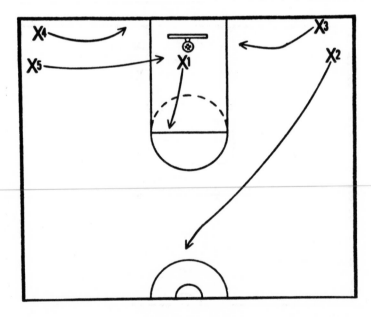

Diagram 4–14b.

percentage. Undoubtedly his conversion percentage was what it was because of his familiarity and ability to execute this option so well.

As the diagram indicates, we simply play "cat and mouse" with the defensive man of X4. As the ball is passed from X2 to X1, X4 steps out as usual, but after a step off his right foot (left foot on the other side of the basket) he cuts off X5. X5 opens immediately to the basket, which could be the beginning of what I call an inside pick-and-roll situation. X5 opens to the basket no matter what the defense does. X4 is looking for the shot, or he will pass to X5 if the defensive switch is used. In the meantime X1 and X2 have split the high post area, even though there is no post man there. After the split, they return to guard positions. At times, we have scored X1 if his defensive man tries to get involved with X4 and the ball. At other times, we have been able to move the ball from X1 to X5 to X4 and back to X1 for the shot.

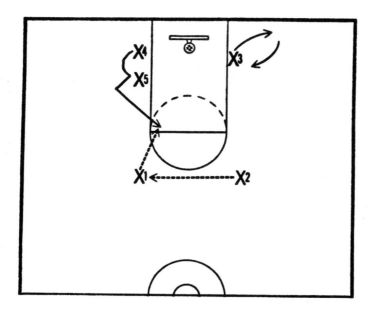

Diagram 4–15.

Guard Around Series

Since this play is considered by many to be the oldest offensive pattern in basketball, it must have some merit if it is still used successfully. For this reason, we have included it in our "Double" offense and realized good results from its usage.

Diagrams 4–16 and 4–17 chart the movement of the guards around by splitting the high post area.

In Diagram 4–16, X2 passes to X1. X4 makes the same step-out and goes to the high post. X1 passes to X4, takes a step forward and provides the screen for X2 as shown. X5 clears the area by going to a double post alignment with X3. If nothing results, X1 and X2 return to guard positions and X4 becomes the weak-side guard. We are then ready to run any phase of the offense again.

In Diagram 4–17, X2 passes to X1 and screens for the latter. X3 starts out straight across the lane and makes a 90-degree turn to come to the high post. X4 has stepped out as always. X1 passes to X3 and drives off the screen of X2. If we gain no advantage, then X4 goes back into double alignment, X1 and X2 return to guard alignments and X3 is again the weakside post man. Again we are ready to move from the double alignment.

How to Perfect the "Destroyer Set"

We drill each option separately in an effort to perfect the offense. It is seldom that we practice the entire offense according to the whole method prior to the passing of three weeks after October 15th. Usually we see the continuity of the offense against a defense in only our three pre-season scrimmage sessions. In addition, perhaps it is worthy of note to mention that we have every player run every position in one half-hour drill once a week; that is, we do so after the first three weeks. In other words, I think it is important that the receiver knows the passer's problems first hand, and vice versa. In the beginning, I think this practice device was silently scorned by our players. In the process of compiling an 18-4 record in one year, many were ready to enjoy the movement of 6-foot, 6-inch Bob Russell as he executed the guard play—and a few grins could be seen. But, within days, we

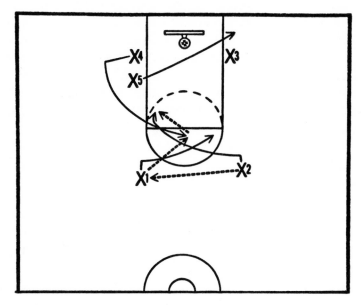

Diagram 4–16.

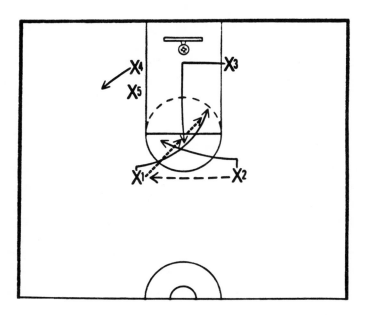

Diagram 4–17.

were amazed at the improvement of Bob's performance in that position. So much so that, later in the season, we used Bob's fine shooting ability on the outside, which forced big defensive men to move out too. So, in a generalized statement, I would like to recommend that every player be drilled occasionally in every position of your offense—whatever the offense may be. If you have never tried it, you might be pleasantly surprised with the results. As a final thought in this regard, Bob Russell's coach was too stupid to use his outside play in the conference championship game one year when we were faced with overwhelming height by Rhode Island College.

Drills to Implement the "Destroyer Set"

Any time we drill our offenses, we do so according to the part method. Since we feel this offense is one of our more important ones, we give it special emphasis during the first three weeks of practice. We do not run the complete offense at any time during that period. We give it emphasis, yes, but only as far as offensive work is concerned. We still spend 70% of our time in the first three weeks on defensive work. This being the case, we must make excellent use of the time remaining. Therefore, we drill each option (five of them) for a total of no more than 15 minutes per practice in the first three weeks. That means we spend about 3 minutes on each option from October 15th to November 6th, 7th or 8th. By the 15th of November, we spend *15 minutes each practice* drilling the entire offense. We do so by walking through it, running it half speed and running it full speed—without a defense. Then we execute it against a defense, which is not allowed to switch or slough at any time. It is drilled against the defense again in phases of walking, half-speed and full-speed movement. Finally we allow the defense to use any methods available to them (other than zones), and again we execute the offense in phases of walking, jogging and full-speed movement. We do not want forced shooting. *We want the shots to happen,* just as passes happen or whatever other *planned things* happen.

Numbering the options, the drills executed are as indicated:

DRILL 1—PICK-AND-ROLL (Diagrams 4–18a and 4–18b)

X4 steps out and receives the pass from a coach. X4 turns around and feeds X5 on the side away from the basket as X5 steps forward to meet it. Then X4 steps back in tight, which gives X5 the opportunity to slice off him. We have two other post men off the floor who in turn run the drill. Each player steps off the floor after completing three executions. At times, we will defense the play of X5 with two freshman ball players. At such times, we do not recognize any foul. In other words, that drill is a blood drill. And we don't want anyone who can't take the contact.

On the other end of the floor, we have the X1 and X2 lines drilling their action and using two managers. We give Mgr. #2 a ball. X2 passes to X1, who in turn passes to Mgr. #1. X1 penetrates and comes off X3 as he steps up the lane. Mgr. #1 looks for X1 and gives him the pass. X1 shoots the jumper. As soon as X1 clears X3, Mgr. #2 passes to X3 who maneuvers for a shot from the post. We feel that two balls and the movements of X1 and X3 help to develop peripheral vision—not just any such vision, but peripheral vision applied to a particular part of the offense.

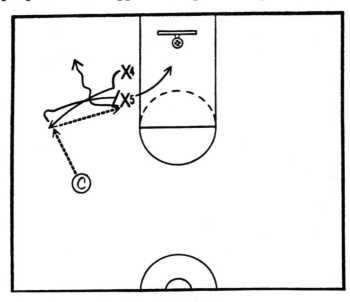

Diagram 4–18a. *Pick-and-roll.*

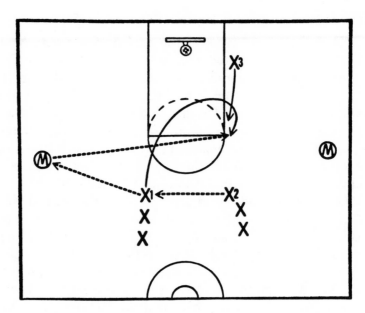

Diagram 4–18b. *Second phase of pick-and-roll.*

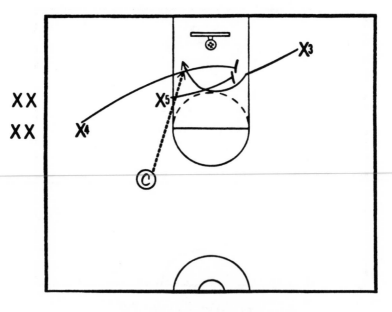

Diagram 4–19. *Double block option.*

DRILL 2—THE DOUBLE BLOCK OPTION (Diagram 4–19)

We drill the double block option trying to score the swing man, as seen in the diagram. We have a coach make the feed pass as the X3, X4 and X5 lines execute the drill. Each player runs each post position several times. Our experience with this phase of the offense indicates there is no problem for the guards to make the feed pass; therefore, we like to have them working elsewhere. Such being the case, the coach passing the ball can give us an accurate observation of the screening ability of the post men as well as their ability to use the screen.

DRILL 3. GUARDS OUTSIDE SHOOTING

Perhaps our outside shooting drill is unique for shooting drills. Actually it was concocted by Coach Bruce Drake when he coached at the University of Oklahoma. I feel it creates pressure while the shooting takes place and therefore simulates game conditions to a degree. I feel a player should practice shooting by taking several shots without interruption. This tends, in my opinion, to get him in the groove better than in drills where the action is interrupted. But I also feel a player should have the second shot only if he is successful with the first. Is this much different than a game situation when a player has a hot hand? I think not. We tend to provide more shooting for that player. Do we want someone shooting who is missing too much? I think not, and therefore he will shoot less in this drill.

In the drill, the winner will be that line of players which makes 21 shots first. The last two baskets must be consecutively made. If a player hits number 20 and then misses number 21, the line must continue until two shots have been made in a row. We find this creates tension and competition in the drill. Each time a shot is made, they must shout out the number. This keeps the other line informed and builds pressure.

This drill tells me how our shooting ability is progressing over the season. The time taken to finish a game of 21 is very indicative of the progress we are making. There certainly is a vast difference in the time it takes to finish a game of 21 in November as compared to one in January. I watch the amount of time taken very carefully, and I make it a point to know who is in that line. Also, I am careful to note who is doing the hitting in that line.

Drill 4. Cat-and-Mouse Option

Drilling the cat-and-mouse option is shown in Diagram 4–20. We have the post men run the spots on both sides of the floor in order to avoid any thinking about the movement as it is being run. It is opportune at this point to revert to theory rather than continue the practical application. I feel players should feel free to use their individual talents within the pattern. That talent is exploited better if they run the offense automatically without feeling their way through it. In the second year of operating the Double offense, we found the team used it without talking about it. This is evidence that meshing of personnel and their peculiar abilities has taken place no matter what their different experiences were prior to playing for Plymouth State.

Either a man in the X1 or X2 position makes the feed pass. X3, X4 and X5 rotate their positions. Post men are obligated to practice right and left hook shots as well as the short jump shots.

Finally, as seen in Diagrams 4–14a and 4–14b, occasionally we will use a corner game from the double alignment. Our use of this alignment is made only when it is certain the defensive man cannot contain the penetration of one of the guards. Sloughing is expected to occur, and appropriate practice time is given to shooting in appropriate areas.

We do not drill the corner game as an offense but merely provide ample practice time to allow our guards to take the ball to the basket. Our daily warm-up drills include such practice, and the way we do it is explained in Chapter 1. We encourage any move by a guard, including behind-the-back dribbling, if he works at it and develops the ability to beat his man. Frankly, I feel that the once-behind-the-back dribble provides an excellent angle for the drive to the basket in 1-on-1 play.

This is what we do in trying to implement the "Destroyer Set" or "Double" offense. I readily agree the offense might be altered and improved as a consequence. Nothing can be static. In fact I am, at the time of this writing, planning a few changes in the offense for future seasons. One of our axioms is that we will use only those elements of the game which have proven to be successful *by our team*. We will not use ideas of others simply because they have been successful for them. In fact I think the

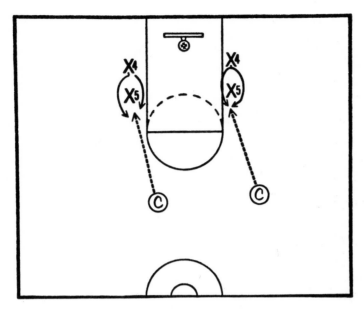

Diagram 4–20. *Cat-and-mouse option drill.*

greatest problem involved with playing winning basketball is how to test ideas before taking the floor for a ball game. I think the best way is to participate in pre-season scrimmages with outside ball clubs, even though these will still not represent true game conditions. The experience of a season, however, can show us where to change plans, and if we work hard enough, how to make them; that is what we have done with the Double offense. We have studied it very carefully after four seasons of play; it has been successful for us. I hope it will be for you, if you decide it is worth your consideration.

Conversion from the "Destroyer Set" to Defense

I believe that the subject of conversion from offense to defense is vital if we are going to win. I also feel that any offensive planning must include defensive preparation to allow us to attack when we lose possession. Yes, we look upon defense as an attack situation. We don't want our opponent to be able to stand back, summarize the situation and then hit us with the best action possible. It is impossible to have a break in the action between operating an offense and organizing to play defense, if you want to be a consistent winner.

As I tried to point out in the beginning of the chapter, we often use the "Destroyer Set" offense if our opponent enjoys a decided height advantage. Although good shooting percentages can be attained in the offense, we also realize that bigger clubs could use a running game against us unless we plan accordingly. We attempt to deny that running game. This thinking dictates that defensive plans must be in effect while running the offense. We make no defensive calls from the bench. The defenses used will depend on how we lose possession. Initially, I thought this would be a very complicated affair. I was proved wrong. All that was involved, as the offense evolved, was to execute the conversion based on two types of missed shots and the turnover. We know we can predict the areas where our shots will be taken. We almost know how the ball will come off the board a great percentage of the time. With this knowledge, we proceeded to plan our defensive efforts for respective occasions.

Against superior height in the post areas and against good defensive rebounding, we implement a man-to-man defense for the post men and ball-you-man for the guards.

If a shot is missed by a guard:

(a) We have the guards assume ball-you-man tactics, and that action must be very aggressive. We attack the man even though he doesn't have the ball. Their men must be in a tough battle of movement. As soon as the opponent has definite possession, two of the post men attack the ball. The third post man drops off in the middle of the floor and goes for the ball wherever it may be—and I mean anywhere—if it were to the opposite end of the floor, he goes for it. Diagram 4–21 depicts a random situation. X5 will always be the middle rebounder. In this case, O3 has possession as X3 attacks on the right side and X5 goes into the double-team effort. Their hands are up with elbows extended out. X1 and X2 take up the ball-you-man alignment on O1 and O2, respectively.

If a shot is missed by a post man:

(b) The guards become the back line in a box zone press. The two post men not involved with the shot become the front line of the zone press, and the man who has the shot will go for the

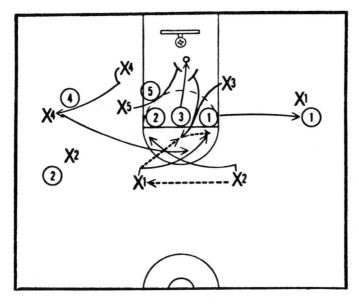

Diagram 4–21.

ball. If the opponent gains possession, the man who shot will hustle to the middle of the zone press making it a 2-1-2 situation. Then we retreat slowly (as slowly as the offense permits) to mid-court while each man is pointing and talking, to and about his man, as we change to man-to-man defense. Diagram 4–22 depicts the situation described.

We are concerned with getting possession through defensive measures more than regaining possession by offensive rebounding. Remember, however, the premise we started from is that the opponent is bigger and has good defensive rebounding ability. In going for the tip-in or the second shot against superior height, we invite foul trouble; therefore, we assure ourselves of good defensive action and try to gain possession through quickness and vigorous defensive action. Frankly, however, if I were accustomed to having four or five players on the bench to replace our front liners, which wouldn't detract from our overall ability, I probably would attack the offensive boards with more enthusiasm. I should also say that this is our plan as we convert from the Double offense. It does not mean we will not crash the boards from other offenses. I must also add that we do not employ the Double of-

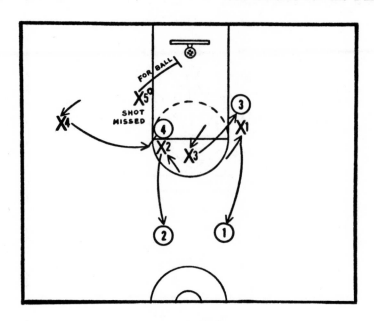

Diagram 4–22.

fense or the type of defense just mentioned if the opposition uses three guards, as far as speed is concerned.

If a turnover occurs (bad pass or any other mechanical error) we retreat to the mid-court area, and we must be running backwards by the time we reach mid-court. At that time, we follow up with whatever defensive plans we want to implement. It is my only objective now to refer myself to the conversion from the "Destroyer Set" or "Double" offense to defense.

II Defensive Complements to the Destroyer

5 • • • • • • • •

How Defensive Changes
in the Game Affect
the Destroyer

The zone presses of the 1950's should have caused more alterations than occurred in man-to-man defensive play. These changes required drills in order to get top-notch execution. Indeed, if we were not aware of the full impact brought to man-to-man defense by the zone presses, how could we concoct drills and eventual satisfactory execution?

In the process of pressuring the offense, the zone presses helped develop better individual and unit offensive play. As a result, it became increasingly more difficult for one defensive man to contain one offensive man in a head-to-head situation. The ball-you-man defense was a natural result. The rotating man-to-man defense may have been another. If you wanted to play man-to-man against improved offensive play, the defense obviously had to improve. In this connection I think I, at least, could have been a better coach in the 50's. The improved offensive play required even better pressure defense to contain the attack. I contend we don't have unit defensive drills to meet improved defensive play *unless we drill in a zone concept. And that is why we are seeing a return to more and more zones.*

I am amused by thinking often expressed which would attempt to legislate the zone defense out of high school and college basketball. From a coaching standpoint, at least, the zone just isn't a legislative matter. What was happening in professional play when Wilt Chamberlain complained about being zoned in the basket area? What was happening when Chamberlain, Russell or Jabbar were roving around in the basket area? Thank goodness only a few people are wasting their time talking about abolishing the zone. The coach who beats the zone will be rid of it.

Conversion from Offense to Defense

A very important phase of playing basketball is converting from offense to defense. The overall better defensive play already mentioned and our increased usage of zone presses brings increased emphasis upon it. I feel our defense must be a part of our offense as plans are made for either phase of the game. It is vital to have the team drilled to convert quickly and efficiently. If you agree that winning is more of a concern of defensive ability than offensive ability, then the first few seconds of adjustment to defense should be a primary factor.

Diagram 5-1 depicts a drill we use to develop the conversion process. Credit must be given to our Assistant Coach, Paul Arold, for his assistance in creating the drill. The "Destroyer Set" or "Double" offense is being drilled in the diagram. As X1 receives the ball, we blow a whistle. The whistle is the signal for whoever has the ball to drop it. Each man retreats toward the mid-court area by running in a straight line. By the time the players reach that area, each must be turned around and pointing at a fictitious opponent. Each will point and shout "mine." The drill is repeated daily for 5 minutes without an opponent until the reaction to the whistle is satisfactory. As we progress the drill is run without the whistle, but the players call the change at any point of drilling the offenses. We want to develop meaningful talk in all phases of the game.

Diagram 5-2 depicts the drill against an opponent. Five men are placed on the base line with a ball. When the whistle is blown, for example while X5 is in possession (again running the

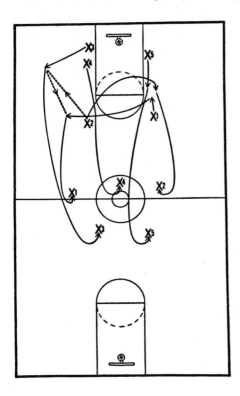

Diagram 5–1.
Conversion from offense to defense drill.

Diagram 5–2.
Conversion from offense to defense drill.

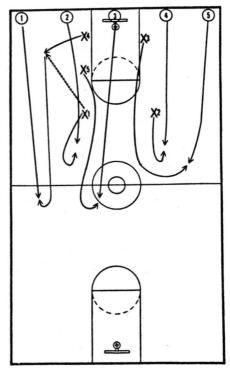

"Double" offense), he drops the ball and the players retreat as shown. Then we blow a second whistle which puts the base line group in action. The time interval between whistles is varied from 1 to 3 seconds until conversion is made very tough.

As shown, X1 is on O2, X4 is on O1, X2 is on O4, X3 is on O5 and X5 is on O3. We use this drill as a part of our efforts to combat fast-breaking ball clubs. In that option of the drill, two guards are moved to outlet pass areas while one of the bigger men attacks the rebounder.

When satisfactory conversion is achieved against the opponent on the base line, we place the two opposing guards in outlet pass areas, but on the sidelines. Two forwards are placed closer to their basket and a post man is positioned on the base line. Diagram 5–3 shows the drill. Obviously, the closer we move the opposition to their basket the tougher the drill will be. We are careful to provide slow progress in the drill. For psychological reasons, we move from the simple to the difficult when placing the opposing five men on the lines. Again from the Double offense we assume a turnover occurs as the ball is passed by X3 to X1. X1 drops the ball on the whistle and the five men retreat. Again the second whistle puts the opposition in motion. We run these conversion drills from any and all of our offenses, zone as well as man-to-man.

Diagram 5–4 indicates a slight deviation in the drill. We assume O1 or O2, or both, have run a "fly pattern" and we need coverage in a hurry. With the ball already this far up the floor, we drill both X1 and X2 (the guards) to turn tail and head for the free throw line—with all-out speed. It is the only time we teach defensive men to have their backs to the ball. At the free throw line, they turn into a tandem alignment. If the ball penetrates that far, the first man will stop the penetration and the second man will cover the first pass. X3 and X5 retreat as fast as possible on the sides while X4 goes to the middle.

Since we like to play patterned offenses, we are able to predict with some accuracy where our players will take their shots and the position of the four other players. With this in mind, a second drill is used which is helpful in converting from shooting situations. Again, the drill is started from any point of our offenses

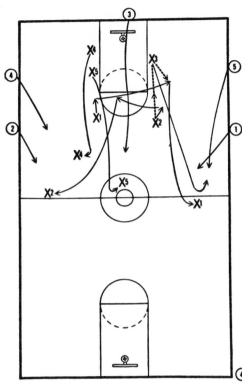

Diagram 5–3.

Conversion from offense to defense drill.

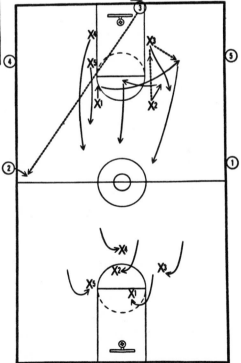

Diagram 5–4.

Conversion from offense to defense drill.

and without opposition. A missed shot is assumed and the ball rebounded by the opposition. In setting the scene, a manager is placed in a random position and conversion is run with the manager having gained possession. Diagram 5–5 shows the drill. The offense is running an option of our "Mike" offense. Assuming X3 misses the shot, the opposition gains possession at position "T." X1 defenses any man in the outlet pass area on the strong side. X2 retreats a bit and will be in the area often used for the second pass of a fast break. X3 and X4 will be involved with the rebound action. Having lost possession, they attack the rebounder to at least prevent the clean outlet pass. X5 retreats deep to the middle of the floor. We are now as seen in Diagram 5–6. If the ball is moved to the opposite side, X1 and X2 take positions as shown.

Diagram 5–7 shows the situation as the ball goes across the floor. In taking the ball across, the offense has lost time in getting the break started. X3 and X4 hustle to mid-court. The ball is now at position "A." After dummy work with the drill, we give it opposition. And we convert from any point of any of our defenses.

Systematic Defensive Variation

Primarily we have used five different defenses: the basic defense is man-to-man, all over the floor; three of them are zone presses and the other is the half-diamond–two defense. The zone presses we use are the 1-2-2, the 2-2-1 and the 3-2. Each of the zone presses are started at a particular part of the floor. We simply use a word to indicate the defensive call. The 1-2-2 is called "point," the 2-2-1 is called "flat," the half-diamond–two is called "ruby" and the 3-2 zone press is called "three." The 1-2-2 and the 2-2-1 are set up at the three-quarter court area while the 3-2 is a mid-court zone press. The man-to-man press is called with words such as "red," "blaze," "fire" or "burn." And we make all defensive calls while playing offense. If we get a bucket from a certain pressing defense, it is a rule that we will be in the same defense after the basket.

The half-diamond–two defense is always aligned in front of the basket without the guards going out very far. If any of these defenses are penetrated, we align in a 1-2-2 zone alignment in the basket area. We do not make such adjustment, of course, when

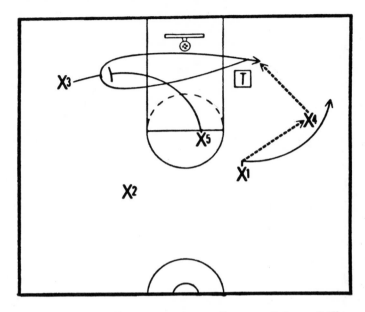

Diagram 5–5. *Converting from offense to defense drill. (Preventing the fast break.)*

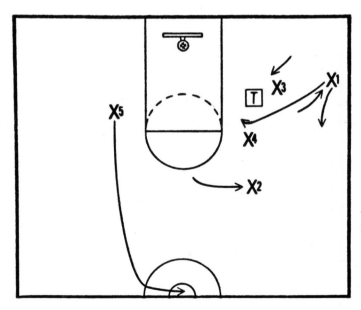

Diagram 5–6. *Converting from offense to defense. (Preventing the fast break.)*

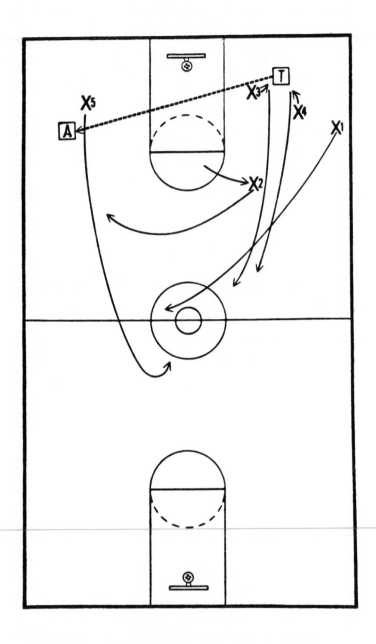

Diagram 5–7. *Converting from offense to defense.*
(Preventing the fast break.)

using the man-to-man press; rather, we stay in that defense. From the 1-2-2 alignment our defenses can be varied, depending on the time the opposition gives us.

Fundamental Considerations in Converting from Offense to Defense

It seems to me that conversion from offense to defense merits consideration of:

1. Pressuring the rebounder with at least one man and at times two men. Our offenses are patterned so that a guard will be about 5 feet from the top of the circle toward the mid-court area. It is his function to shut off an outlet pass from a rebounder to the area. This, in turn, allows a corner man to either double-team the rebounder or take position in the outlet pass area laterally. In any case, all players challenging the rebounder must do so with arms high.

2. Alternating the conversion from dropping back, as in Diagrams 5-1 and 5-3, to attacking, as indicated above.

3. Seeing everything we can of the opposition and then talking our heads off to help one another get into the defensive pattern we are using.

4. Developing retreat lanes from our offense, which have been diagrammed in Diagrams 5-1, 5-2, 5-3 and 5-4. We retreat in this fashion from all our offenses, including our corner game.

6 • • • • • • • • •

How to Develop Tough Man-to-Man Defense

Perhaps our use of the "Destroyer Offense," involving sideline play, does cause us to try to play better defense in the perimeter areas.

The concern we have for sideline play has caused us to be very careful that the language we use is completely understood by our club. One very important term used in our defensive jargon is concerned with the out-of-bounds line. There is only one line, one term—the base line. We just don't use the term "sideline." If a defensive man is beaten on the outside, anywhere on the floor, the man beating him is going to the end of the floor— the base line. Therefore, for us, the entire playing area is enclosed by a *base line*. If this seems trivial, I should remind you it has helped us instill better defensive concentration in each man playing defense. This has been true when using zone presses, traditional zones, man-to-man defenses or combinations of both. We protect that base line energetically. We do so at mid-court as well as at the end of the floor. Although we try to place a certain amount of emphasis on shoulder alignment between the offensive and the defensive men, we are still emphasizing base line play. If I am repetitious, it is because I am in the habit of repeating the idea so often to our players throughout every season. This explanation notwithstanding, I have used the term "sideline" frequently in this book, since I don't want to hinder the reader by forcing him to check the use of terms any more than necessary.

Playing good defense is keynoted by an aggressive attitude, in ways which enable defensive men *to help one another.* I have never seen a good or certainly a great ball club which didn't include players who helped one another in the execution of their defenses. All of their defenses were "helping defenses." It may have involved just "switching" or "sloughing." But usually it had to do with all phases of defensive play, individually and collectively.

Aggressiveness, then, is the number one characteristic most worthy of development in defensive play. Winning basketball games is a question of playing good defense. Consistent winning cannot be achieved without it. We hate to lose. And when we do lose, we can nearly always point out the fact that aggressiveness was lacking. I don't believe in relying on luck. Being in the right place at the right time can be achieved by using successful tactics —tactics proven under game conditions to be successful. Then the tactics must be drilled, drilled and drilled some more. My definition of luck is: aggressively drilled execution of detailed planning. Aggression creates luck on the floor.

Despite the fact that there will be those coaches who will disagree with me (and successful they may be), I don't believe a player can play sound defense if he is not sound in the fundamentals of man-to-man play. The reason is simple. In the seconds of the feed pass or the shot, even within a zone, the defense is of a man-to-man nature. I recognize that two or even more defensive men can be involved, but often it is a 1-on-1 situation. How can a lad not oriented to 1-on-1 play be expected to execute defensive play satisfactorily when required to do so within a zone? Therefore, we assume that 1-on-1 defensive play is the base upon which we must build.

Our defensive preparation is based on the premise, "A good offensive man will beat a good defensive man in 1-on-1 play." I buy that concept. But buying it and accepting it are two different things. Every practice session we run includes efforts to make it untrue. I readily agree there are areas of our approach which can be justly criticized if taken out of context. But we do certain unique things which support the overall approach. And they produce success.

It isn't a function of this book to deal with team defensive play of the man-to-man variety, but I would be remiss if I didn't at least mention the individual fundamentals we execute. Some of those factors are:

1. Defensive stance. The outside foot is back, knees bent, the body slightly turned to the base line and the base line hand is open in a low-to-the-floor position. The front hand is held about belt high, ready to move upward to bother the outside shot. We want this hand moving constantly.

2. We concentrate our eyes on the opponent's belt line. (Hip movement is the key to all body movement.)

3. Whenever an offensive man, in possession of the ball, turns his back to the basket, we try to attack him with a second man. This is a variable, depending on the ability of the opposing post man to move the ball.

4. Each player must holler "shot" when the man he is working on shoots. I feel it is psychologically dangerous to shout "take it, shoot" or "you've got it." If the shooter hits, he can turn such talk to his psychological advantage.

5. The defense must attack. We teach the attack by using the boxer's movement. It is sound practice early in the season to have players pair off and let them go through the boxing movement.

6. The defensive man must make the offensive man react to defensive movement. The defense must move before the offense does so; it isn't a simple thing to teach, but the results are worth the effort. The aggressive attitude we seek is helped by this work. Further, I think it rubs off on all phases of play.

7. We try to build pride through defensive efforts. Hustle, good conditioning and ability to execute a few basic ideas are the backbone of pride.

As a team, we try to follow these rules while operating man-to-man defense:

1. If you are "off the ball," open to the ball.

2. If you are "on the ball," attack.

3. If you are "weak side"–front line, drop to the lane.

4. If you are "strong side"–back line and off the ball; play heavy toward the base line.

5. Always defense the post man on the ball side when he is not in the lane.

6. Get in front of the post man if he is within 8 feet of the basket and not in possession.

7. If your man is in possession and turns his back to the basket, back off a step and holler for help.

Our practice includes considerable time given to 1-on-1 defensive drills. I become very irritated if a player exhibits the attitude that he already knows and can execute the drills. Newcomers and returning lettermen must execute the defensive drills with equal enthusiasm. Unfortunately, I find ball players coming out of high schools are weaker and weaker in 1-on-1 play. Our 1-on-1 drills are slugfests. If the players are in good physical condition, there is no need to worry about overwork in this phase of preparation. We have a coach supervising the drills who corrects errors as they happen. And we like to have coaches leave practice with hoarse voices, myself included.

It doesn't make sense that good or excellent shooters should spend so much time in shooting practice as is often the case. Time must be given to maintain or improve that ability, but many young players would benefit if some of this time were spent on defensive work.

Defensive Talk

Since meaningful talk is such a big part of playing good defense, talking is a necessary ingredient in all our drills. Players not running the drills momentarily are made to talk from the sideline. If players running the drills aren't talking, then the players on the sideline must get them to do so. From a talking standpoint, this improves both those on the floor and those on the sideline.

Defensive Shoulder Alignment

Up to the free throw line and the line extended, we want the defensive man's outside shoulder to be aligned on the offensive man's inside shoulder. From the free throw line and the line extended to the basket, we want the defensive man's inside shoulder to be aligned on the offensive man's outside shoulder.

I took this defensive idea from Coach Hank Iba a few years ago and it is a tremendous help. Such guidance to our defense helps to protect the head of the circle—a critical jump shooting area—and still protects the outside from the free throw line to the basket. So many offenses today jam the area at the head of the circle, that we intend to deny some of that shooting. Diagram 6–1 shows the idea.

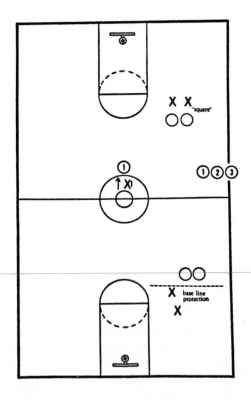

Diagram 6–1. *Defensive shoulder alignment.*

Over the Top

While running man-to-man defenses, we make every effort to have the defensive man go "over the top" every time his man tries to brush him on a teammate. *We don't want players who don't relish contact, and this is one of the plays where we find out who likes contact.* Quick and violent contact is the objective. The man making the move must do so low-to-the-floor and actually make room for himself. He beats the offensive man to the top position, arms in front of him with the elbows bent. *A "take charge of my man" attitude is vital.* We'll take our chances with the referees' whistles.

In mid-court drills, we don't allow two men to get between a defensive man and the man he is playing. It is possible that I make a mistake in not *requiring* every man to "go over the top" every time. Notice I said we make *every effort* to do so, but it is not always required. In a sense I am wrong in that all that is required to do so is all-out aggression, good physical conditioning and some knowledge. On the other hand, the jamming offenses might make defensive men vulnerable to the jump shot at the head of the circle, even if they get over the top. I can only say that I am constantly weighing this situation.

Sliding

Many times this maneuver is an excuse for not "going over the top." We accept it reluctantly only because of factors mentioned in the previous paragraph and because some screening-weaving teams, in my opinion, do prevent "over the top" movement sometimes. It must not become the rule but rather the exception.

Two factors seem to be paramount in sliding. The man "on the ball" must talk, and we have him shout one word, "room," as he goes through, next to the ball. The man "off the ball" answers "okay." The reply of "okay" reminds the "off the ball" man to pull his forward leg back, which will allow room for his teammate to slide through without collision.

1-on-1 Drills

The drills are started at mid-court. Sometimes we do so without a ball while offensive men move where and when they please as the defensive men take boxer jabs at them and recover. Here we insist "You gotta dance." As they jab forward with the front leg, they must dance back as quickly as possible . . . as soon as that front foot hits the floor. Everything is done to prevent the offensive man from closing to the defensive man. Efforts are made to keep 2 feet of daylight between them. But there will be seconds when the defensive man is tight if he is attacking the ball correctly. Frankly there are times when our players get caught going the wrong way, but when it happens we notice they are almost always freshmen or sophomores. An incident which pleases me is the occasional backward fall of a defensive man as he kicks off his front foot to recover quickly in backward movement. It means he is working to master such quick footwork that he can't maintain his equilibrium. In time he will. Proper footwork can be learned.

2-on-2 Drills

The procedure is the same. We may begin with no ball. Offensive men are told to move where they will on the floor. The defensive men are dictated to, raved at and repeatedly drilled in the various phases of defensive execution. We don't talk about "switching, sliding or sloughing" in front of a blackboard, we do it on the floor. We stop the action when we want to explain or correct the play. We take whatever time necessary to achieve desired results. No error is too small for correction. And we allow no talk other than defensive talk from anyone. The only talk heard above the din should be our own raving.

3-on-3 Drills

A third pair of players is added to the mid-court drill. The same procedures are used, but we add one or two other factors. We have both men "off the ball" open to the ball, each trying to tend toward "ball-you-man" shape. If a defensive man is two men away from the ball he goes into a slough, while the man adjacent to the ball takes definite "ball-you-man" shape. Diagram 6–2 depicts the alignments. In area 1, both X3 and X1 tend to "ball you man" shape because both are adjacent to it. In area 2, X3 has sloughed toward the middle, X2 is in pronounced "ball you man" shape and X1 is attacking. In other words, ball movement is denied; force the offense to base line movement and then be quick enough to refuse access to that line. The impasse is frustrating to the offense.

Five minutes every practice, all defensive men put their hands behind their backs while going through the defensive drills. When working with a ball, we allow the offensive men to double

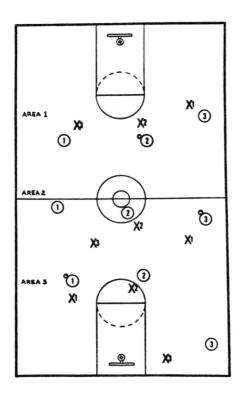

Diagram 6–2. *Defensive alignment in 3-on-3 drills.*

dribble or do whatever they can as we stress defensive execution. Someone once remarked that maybe I helped players learn to double dribble. If I have ever seen anyone learn to double dribble, the habit was broken during our pre-season scrimmages, because it is a rare call made by officials in our ball games.

Defensing the Post

It just plain irritates me to have an opponent in possession take position close to the basket with his back to it. Since nearly all ball clubs use a low post or two, I am irritated all the time. But I try to ease my irritation.

We defense the post men on either side of the lane from the "ball side" position. Although it is very tough, we sometimes try to front the high post and we always front the low post. But let's face it, actual fronting of the high post is achieved effectively very few times, unless we use second-man help in back of the post. Most of the time we are heavy to the strong side before the post man has possession and in back when he is in possession. We always want to see another man trying to help out from the other side or in front. Opposing guards are usually too quick to run the risk of dropping off out front. Opposing guards are the people most able to move the ball and shoot long. Consequently, we drop off elsewhere—in the weakside corner area. Diagram 6–3 deals with the situation.

X5 has primary responsibility to O2, and he should be involved with O5 if he gets the ball and comes to the weak side. If the ball does go to O5, we drop X2 toward O3. If the ball moves across the floor, we adjust by moving X2 all the way to the O3 area. X3 moves to the lane and may become a "rover," unless O3 moves out, in which case X3 will go with him and X2 is in a helping position. At any rate this is a simple adjustment of the weakside corner man dropping to the deep post area. If either O3 or O4 move through and out of the area, we must play honest by engaging them with X2 and X3. If O3 and O4 remain in the weakside area and the ball goes back to the middle as in Diagram 6–4, X5 takes up the slack and engages O2. Now X3 would reverse to be the helper in the post situation, if the ball is on the front line—center position. And while the ball is in such location, everyone

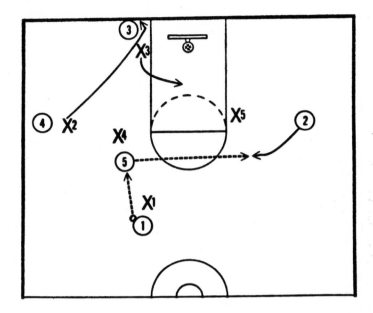

Diagram 6–3. *Dropping off in the weakside corner.*

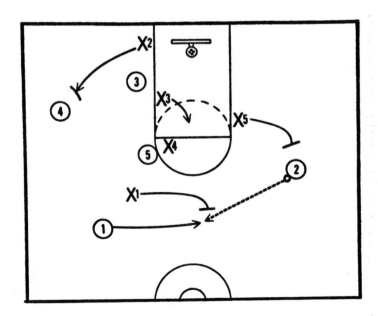

Diagram 6–4. *Helping the defensive post play.*

would play honest if the offense fills the corners, except X3, as he may supply help with the low post.

Defensing the Feed Pass

I feel we overlook an important phase of defense in that not enough pressure is brought to the passer. This means we might try to deny clean release of the ball at least in one direction. By doing so, we allow cleaner release in another direction. The effort I like to execute calls for "ball you man" shape on the ball as well as off of it. If the four men "off the ball" play really aggressive defense, the fact that we play to one side of the man with the ball should not be that dangerous. Playing heavy to one side of the ball steers movement in the direction we want our opponents to go. We can steer it to our advantage. For example, playing strong on the side of a would-be passer who is an outstanding performer about to pass the ball to a man who is slower and less able than his defensive man, would be advantageous. If we are convinced the offense is hard put to beat our defense in 1-on-1 situations, we will align and play "ball you man." Diagram 6–5 shows another random case. O1 is in possession. X2 aligns strong toward O1, leaving himself open to penetration by O5 (if O5 goes, X2 must go). If O1 is dead (used his dribble), we want X1 to align on one side or the other of that man. And, as mentioned, under certain circumstances we will align on him to one side or the other, even if he has not dribbled. If O1 penetrates on the dribble, the basic rotation rules are executed of which there are four:

(1) Strong-side defense opens to the ball and has his back to the base line.

(2) Weakside guard rotates to the middle.

(3) Defensive post stops penetration.

(4) Weakside corner rotates to the same side as open offensive man.

Diagram 6–5 shows the movement continuing from Diagram 6–4. O4 nearly always reacts to the release by X3 by going to the base line. Therefore, X1 hustles to that area and is looking for an interception on the way. At times, X1 can wheel around and trap

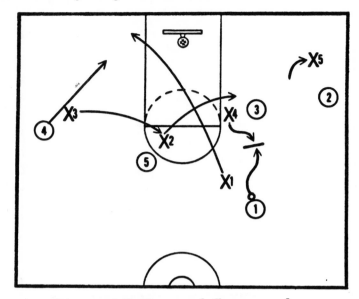

Diagram 6–5. *Five-man ball-you-man shape.*

the ball as O1 is on the way in. X4 must stop the penetration far enough out to deny the good jump shot in the circle area. I must add that we do not try this execution if both guards are above average in talent.

Defensing the Weakside Drive

An important consideration in playing good defense involves defensive execution away from the ball. We all know and demand such play, but sometimes we don't get satisfactory execution because we are just talking when we should be drilling. *We drill it.*

If the man adjacent to the ball plays tough ball-you-man defense, we don't have to worry about defensive play away from the ball. Since we are not always using that defensive concept, we have to be concerned. The phase of defense involved with weakside play centers on the second and third men from the ball. As I have tried to describe elsewhere, we have the second and third men go into a slough movement if the offense stands around enough to permit it. Again, if we played tight defense every night, it would not be so vital to concern ourselves with weakside play. Sloughing deals with our basic premise that the good of-

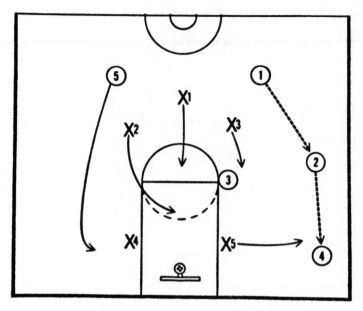

Diagram 6–6. *Defensing the weakside drive.*

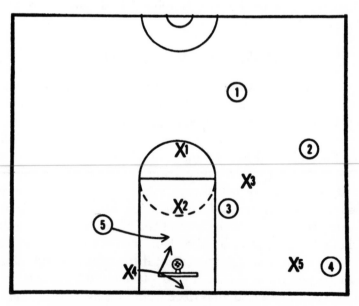

Diagram 6–7. *Defensing the weakside drive.*

fensive man will beat the good defensive man in a 1-on-1 situation. We slough to introduce a helping aspect into our defenses; therefore, the weakside drive is of concern. Sloughing invites weakside play, which usually means driving toward the ball and the basket—the offense must react that way.

Diagram 6–6 gets into the matter. O1 has the ball. O1 passes to O2. O5 has ideas about "back dooring" our 1-2-2 zone. O2 passes to O4. X5 engages O4. X3 drops to front O3. X1 drops into the circle. X2 goes into the lane. X4 is now in a tough spot, unless he is drilled to handle the weakside drive by O5. The action we want from X4 is not taken for granted.

X4 must open to the ball and to O5. Diagram 6–7 shows X4's position as well as those of the rest of the defense. If O5 goes all the way to the base line, then X4 must get to that line. The arrows ⌐→ indicate the position of X4's hands, and we insist that he point to O5 and O4 with them. By pointing his hands, the player will tend to develop the peripheral vision necessary to do the job. The real test of that vision comes as O5 moves through the lane. *As O5 starts,* X4 takes a step or two toward the lane. This closes him to the ball a bit and helps him read O5's intentions. He must still follow the adage "Don't give up the base line," because we have no help there. So, if O5 does go toward the line, X4 must back up accordingly. Again, X4 is in a tough spot were it not for the position of the ball. X5 and the superstructure of the backboard make it impossible to throw a pass to O5, unless, and until, the latter is on the same side of the basket as the ball.

As O5 moves more toward the free throw lane, X4 must move so that his position in the lane is as shown in Diagram 6–7. In other words, the more the distance between the ball and O5 decreases, the more X4 opens to the ball. But we don't say "front" O5. We explain and drill *how we want him to do it.* I consider this a very dangerous situation. Ball movement in that area must be hotly contested. And I believe it is this type of defensive play which detracts a great deal from otherwise good defensive teams.

X4 plays an important "cat and mouse" game with O4. X4 must key on the passer as he opens to the ball. X4 should also try to fake movement in an effort to cause a faulty reaction by O4. If the reverse happens, we may see the ball dropped into the basket by O5 and a foul shot following the 2 points.

In Diagram 6–8, X2 has dropped off toward O5 if the pass is thrown by O4, but we couldn't do this in the man-to-man game. Also, as mentioned, if 05 moves across the lane X4 must go with him, since that overload against any of our zones calls for man-to-man action within the zone. Yes, you can take us out of the zone by overloading, but as soon as you unload (and you must move if we go to man-to-man on the people doing the overloading), we will return to the zone with ease.

Diagram 6–9 continues the action from Diagram 6–8 and shows the action in response to the overload-underload movements. O5 moves as shown. X4 stays. Assuming O4 passes to O2, X3 engages and X5 drops off. X2 is thinking about O3. With the pass to O2, X4 drops off closer to the basket than X5, but he is also ready to return if the ball reverses back to O5. If the ball moves to O1, X4 and X5 both return to their slots in the 1-2-2 zone.

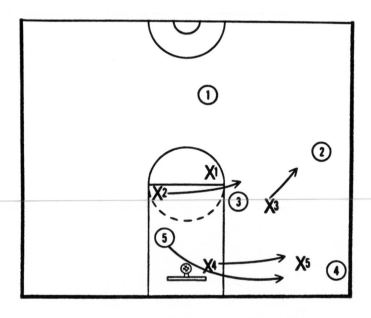

Diagram 6–8. *Defensing the weakside drive.*

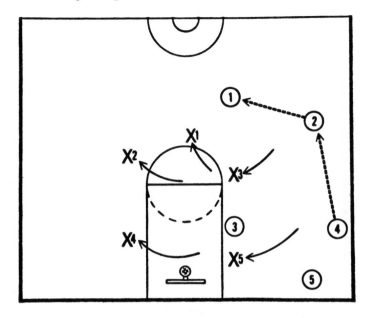

Diagram 6–9. *Defensing the weakside drive.*

Weakside Drive Defensive Drill

The most dangerous place on the floor where the weakside drive can happen is in the area shown in Diagrams 6–8 and 6–9. Therefore, we drill the movement desired in that area. In addition, the drill is run in the free throw line area; and we drill it on both sides of the lane.

In Diagram 6–10, O1 passes to O2, O2 lobs the ball to the manager and O5 starts to jockey for the weakside drive toward the ball. X4 executes the movement already described, and a coach is under the basket to assure correct execution. In order to run the drill at the free throw line, we just move O5 to that area and all others adjust accordingly. A second phase of the drill is that which finds the overload already achieved and not in the movement process. This drill is shown in Diagram 6–11.

Now five men are used because the entire defense must react to the movement of the ball. We maintain the drill helps in execution of zones or man-to-man action. The five-man drill includes man-to-man execution against weakside drives; therefore, we are

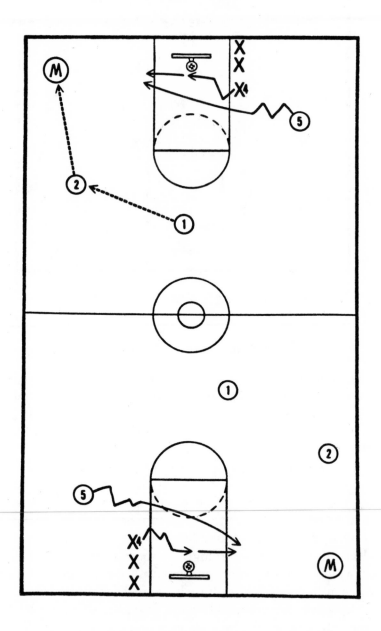

Diagram 6–10. *Defensing the weakside drive drill.*

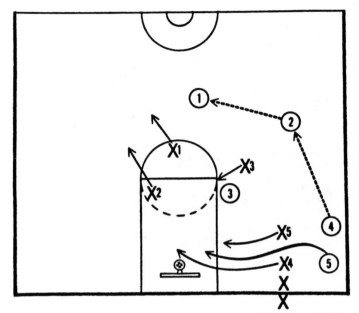

Diagram 6–11. *Defensing the weakside drive drill.*

really drilling for any of our defenses except the ball-you-man effort. The drill is clumsy since five men repeatedly return to starting points. The drill should be run at least five times in a set. Our attention throughout the drill is riveted to the defensive actions of X5 and X4, while that of X4 is the key action of the two.

7 • • • • • • • • • •

How to Get
Good Usage of
Zone Presses

Our use of zones includes a few zone presses and a traditional zone. From that traditional zone, we make several defensive changes. Although zone presses will now be discussed, it is appropriate to include some other defenses since they are integrated into the overall plan of zone press usage. If the zone presses are penetrated up the floor, we set up in a 1-2-2 zone in front of the basket. Often we stay in that zone and work accordingly. At other times, the 1-2-2 will change to man-to-man. Whatever our defense, we attack just as one thinks of attacking offensively. Attack leads to aggression and we want aggressive people.

Consistent winning cannot be achieved today by using just man-to-man defenses. Certainly whatever success we have had has been due, in part, to use of zone presses and traditional zones. Our idea is to become as tough as possible in man-to-man efforts, put in a few zone presses and become very efficient with one traditional zone. The problems ensuing primarily have been concerned with gaining the fluid change from one to another. We align in a way which best permits us to execute any one of three or four defenses. It is a dangerous game, and we have been caught at times in going from one to another. Nevertheless, if we can get the opposition accustomed to certain defensive patterns, all coming from the same starting point, we may be able to run a defense they do not smell out readily.

It may be helpful if I explain part of a typical defensive game plan. First, we often start a ball game playing man-to-man, all over. Traps are used where they can be had. Many times the offense will clear out and give their best ball handler the opportunity to bring the ball up the floor. He usually does so successfully. He dribbles a lot and five men are not meshing offensively. After a few minutes of such offensive play, we change to a zone press. Sometimes the offense will continue to be "on the ball" a little bit too much. At that point, we sometimes gain turnovers and occasionally an insurmountable lead. Inevitably the offense will adjust successfully, but we have tried to seize whatever lead possible in the interim. Even if this isn't the case, we gain one advantage, which is to take a running game away from them. Getting a running game going isn't easy when one man is bringing the ball up the floor.

When the zone press hits them, errant passes may occur. They are in a hurry to move the ball. Now the press is more effective and turnovers can be had before they calm down. Before that time, we may have a 4-15 point lead. If we don't have enough savvy, discipline and talent to win with a 7-point lead (remember we are a club that will run patterns patiently), then we probably don't figure to win anyway.

There have been times when we could play man-to-man out of a 1-2-2 zone alignment simply because the offense didn't penetrate. This makes for defensive play in a restricted area.

Predicting the Score Before the Game Is Played

I try to figure the final score of the game before it is played. It is possible to calculate a range and then adjust plans accordingly. This must be a prediction based on facts as much as possible and not on hopes. If a tight game or a losing effort seems certain, some changes might prevent unsatisfactory results—

namely, losing. Knowledge of opposing personnel, their coach's way of playing the game, our own talent and many other factors can be important. In some cases, we placed unusual responsibility on certain players, played slow-down basketball, used defenses we had never drilled and adjusted in other ways. And, quite frankly, I admit that in rare cases we weren't going to be in the ball game despite our best efforts. This has allowed me to sleep better, work harder and generally be more effective.

Trapping in Zone Presses

Before discussing each zone press we use, it is necessary to talk about "traps." We apply the traps the same way in all our zone presses.

As a young fox hunter I had occasion, years ago, to be just out of range for a shot with a shotgun, which kept me from having a pelt of old Raynard. My youthful zest caused me to break out in a dead run at such times, in a straight line toward the animal. Invariably, he would run away at whatever angle necessary to gain good cover. Good cover was his objective rather than distance. Those fox hunting experiences carry a lesson for me as we try to apply traps in our zone presses. The man about to be trapped in basketball will run for cover too. If not careful, we may chase him to the middle, where the ball will leave him to gain the cover of his teammates' hands. Or, if we go at him head-on, he may head for the spectators as we do. Maybe he'll use the sideline as an escape hatch. *Whatever the case, he'll go somewhere fast if we go at him head-on fast.* If he goes for that base line too fast, he may get to it and through it before we can head him off. If we chase him to the middle, he may be looking down our throats in a good fast-break situation.

The first trap is one from which we seldom gain much advantage. Seldom does a turnover occur. What we want is a series of traps, and in the series of traps turnovers are produced. Diagram 7–1 shows a trap from our "point" defense. As O1 moves the ball to O2, X2 takes on sideline responsibility of containment. X1 approaches the trap with stealth, not speed. We want him to run parallel to O2's movement and go for the trap when only a step or two from O2. If X1 runs straight at the ball, he often will

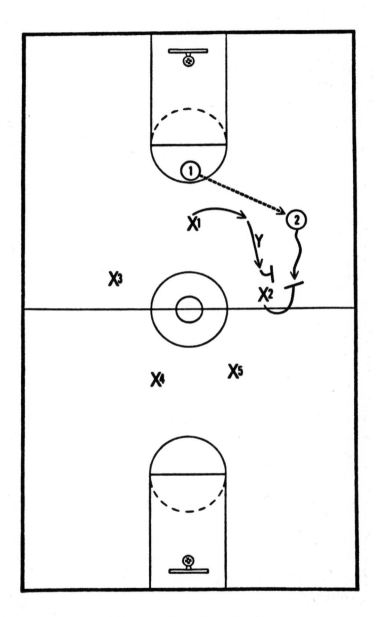

Diagram 7–1. *Trapping.*

chase the man rather than trap him. His man will react as the fox did. Only, in this case, the pelt is the ball and it will be passed to better cover. We don't want him to release quickly. That's one way to beat the trap—by means of quick, accurate ball movement. Line "Y" shows the parallel movement of X1 related to O1. A second or two prior to containment by X2, X1 will set his path for a collision course with O1.

The traditional trap as described is probably the way most teams execute it. But our plan in applying a second trap from the first one is different. The item of our plan which varies is the sixth one in our guidelines for trapping:

(1) Maintain slightly flexed knee position.

(2) Extend the arms as high as possible.

(3) Don't go for the ball.

(4) Prevent "splitting" or sideline penetration at all costs.

(5) Cause a lob pass or a bounce pass.

(6) Turn your back to the ball if leaving one trap to go to another.

Execution of number six above is in keeping with the lesson learned from the fox hunt. In Diagram 7–3, X3 can contain O4. If so, X3 seeks to bring O4 back toward the middle by a step or two. O4 will be very aware of players in back of him. The lesson learned from the fox is that the man in the trap, which has been sprung, must leave the area *with his back to the ball*. Don't run right at the fox—I mean the ball. The ball will be moved too quickly if you do so. X2 comes toward the middle a step or two, not looking at the action of X3 and O4. X2 wheels suddenly and applies the second half of the second trap. O4 will be able to pass to O2 with no problem. In that event we rarely get a turnover, but we do get turnovers if O4 passes the ball toward the basket. (The diagram shows a "turnover" with a back court violation.) However, if we don't get a turnover, so what? What have we lost? The opposition is moving the ball away from their basket. I like that. The point stressed is that we leave one trap to execute another, by having the man closest to the ball moving with his back to the man he is going to trap.

Steering the ball in zone presses is an important part of the trapping process. We try to do so as early as possible. Someone effects point play to achieve that early steering. Even in the "flat" front line pressing zone (2-2-1), one of the front line players

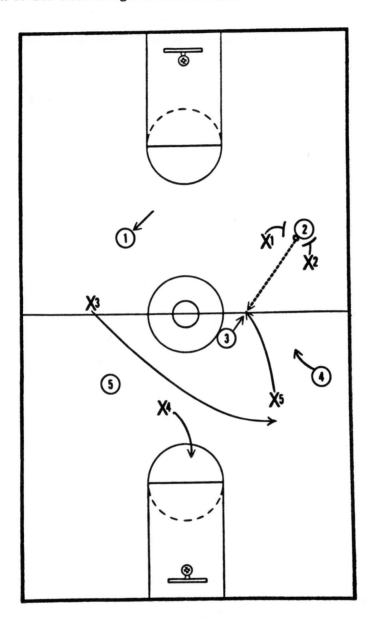

Diagram 7-2. *Going for the ball out of the trap.*

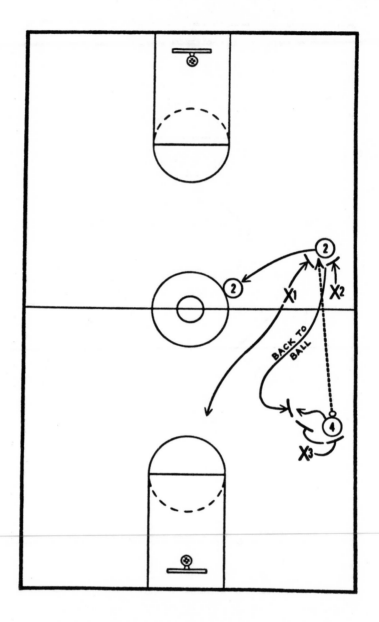

Diagram 7–3. *Moving from one trap to another.*

must give us an early indication of ball movement. If they are forced to the sideline, the offense will try to move the ball toward the middle if given half a chance. In Diagram 7–2, the ball would be passed to O3. By steering the ball, we put ourselves in a calculated risk situation to cover that pass. We go for the ball in a specific area and with one man. We feel it is a serious mistake to go for that pass with two men. X4 can't have a good chance for the ball because he is too far away and has a bad angle on it. X5 has the angle of interception and uses it. In Diagram 7–2, possession by O4 would place us in jeopardy. We are very definite in assigning X3 with the responsibility of dealing with the situation. X5 shouts X3's name, which means he is going for the ball. This forces X3 to move as shown. If our trap is effective and if O2 is made to hesitate a bit and then passes to O4, we may have a turnover by X3. X4 backs off to the head of the circle. If the ball goes back to O1 from O2, we feel we have lost nothing. X5 has interchanged with X3. X5 must beat O1 to the sideline if the latter chooses to go there. We drill this from either side of the floor, of course. And the drills are done under scrimmage conditions. Diagrams 7–4 and 7–5 show the situation if the ball goes back across the floor. Essentially we are in a 1-2-2 zone, and we will trap again if O1 tries to penetrate as he is chased away from the sideline by X5.

Relieving Back Line Pressure

The team must have confidence that the opposition cannot throw the ball over the back line of our zone presses; the front line play will be more aggressive if this confidence exists. It can be demonstrated it isn't possible by allowing anyone to try to do so without defensive pressure on them as the ball is thrown. A drill we use to develop the confidence mentioned is shown in Diagram 7–6. O1 and O2 attempt to throw the ball over the heads of X5 and X4, respectively. We ask, no, we order, that X5 and X4 try to get in a straight line between the ball and any opponent to their rear. Their hands are ready to be raised over their heads. Their feet should be placed in such a way as to allow them to see the ball and the man to the rear. It is a man-to-man situation. If, however, the ball should reach O4, for example, X4 would

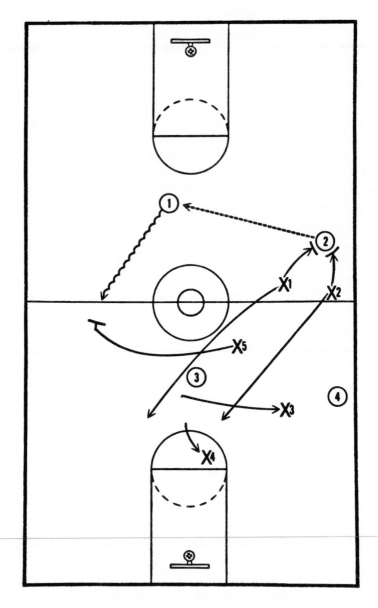

Diagram 7–4. *Reverse defensive flow from trap.*

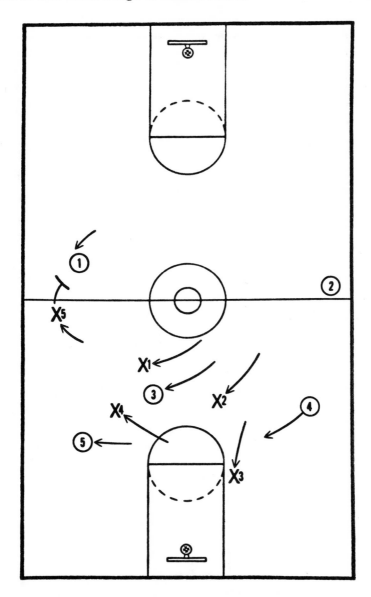

Diagram 7–5. *Reverse defensive flow from trap.*

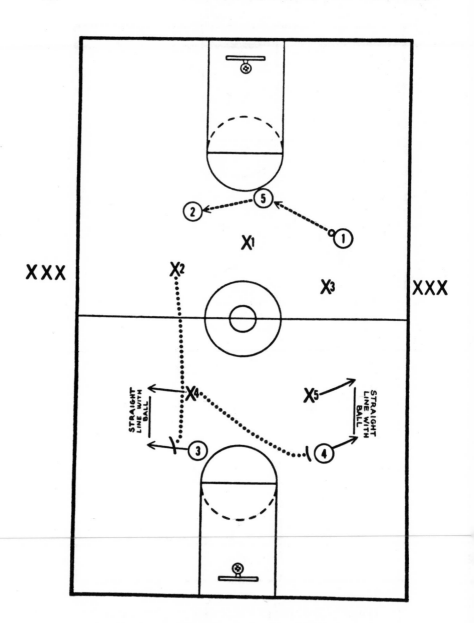

Diagram 7–6. *Relieving back line pressure in zone presses.*

immediately help out. As the dotted lines indicate, both X4 and
X2 would help out. The reverse would be true if the ball reaches
O3. We also orient the entire defense to be aware of the would-be
passer's feet. If he has one foot in front of the other, he is in position to throw the long baseball pass. The more his feet are parallel,
the less possibility there is he can throw that pass.

Diagram 7–7 shows back line movement as the ball approaches the mid-court line. As the ball comes toward the line,
X4 and X5 drop off toward the basket. As a guideline, the back
line men are taught to drop back one step for each two steps
forward of the offensive men in their own back court. They do so
in relation to the ball only, not in relation to men without the
ball. Experience has shown us that the one step for two steps ratio
is sound. This is undoubtedly helped by the front line defense
wielding strong pressure on the ball when opposing guards are in
possession.

Of course the height factor is an important consideration in
such action. If confronted by a 7-footer in the lane area, we would
need a different plan. Putting the situation in perspective, however, the back line play does not suffer when using two 6-foot,
5-inch boys against opposing heights ranging from 6 feet, 2 inches
to 6 feet, 8 inches. The bigger the opposition, the more tempting
it is to throw a lob pass. We have enjoyed good success in this
phase of our zone presses. As mentioned though, anything above
6 feet, 8 inches probably would call for an adjustment. We drill
this action using five men, in a minimum set of five repetitions.

The 1-2-2 Zone Press

Our first objective with the defense is to steer ball movement
to one side or the other. *We don't want the ball in the middle of
the floor.* When possible, the "point man" tries to move the man
with the ball to the side away from the opponent's dominant arm.
Diagram 7–8 shows the alignment. Actually, all five men are free
to move toward the base line if the "point man" does so, but we
prefer to start with the three-quarter floor alignment. If the opposition develops a case of nerves, then we will move the defense
to the base line and exert pressure on the man trying to throw the
ball in play.

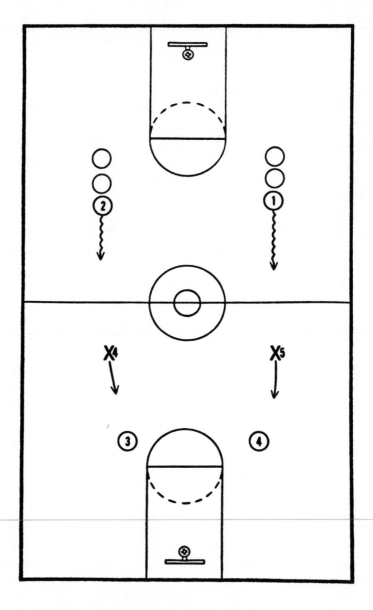

Diagram 7–7. *Relieving back line pressure in zone presses.*

X1 gives us ball movement on O2. X2 assumes sideline containment responsibility. X3, X4 and X5 move as shown. If X2 contains O3, X1 should react in a way to complete the trap as explained in the section on trapping. The play of X5 is now critical. If O2 should break the trap with a dribble, he must stop his progress. If the ball comes out of the trap via a pass, X5 must be ready to go for the ball. If the opposition puts a man on the sideline, to the right of him, we take some of the pressure off X5 by telling him to stress play on that man. In such case X3 is automatically the man who will go for the ball, if a pass is made by O2 to O4. If the opposition does not have a man in the sideline area, near X5, obviously it changes our effort to get the ball. In this case, we want X5 to go for the ball. X3 will then exchange spots with X5 as in Diagram 7–9. If the offense takes position in the area just vacated by X5, X3 must go wide enough to deny the base line to the man going there. X3 will remain, however, just as close to the middle of the floor as O5 (probably O5) will allow. X4 goes to the middle of the floor.

We try to trap the ball from this defense whenever it goes to a corner. Diagram 7–10 shows a typical action situation. Assuming O3 has passed to O5 and the latter dribbles toward the corner, X1 and X2 must start hustling as soon as the trap they applied is broken. X3 must play cute; he should try to tempt O5 to go for the basket but at the same time make very sure he can't get there. The man in the middle, X4, becomes the second man in the trap. X5 remains on the front line to close off an "out pass" by O5 to the front line area. X1 and X2 play in a way that shuts off the "honey play," as we call it. That idea is explained as follows.

Shutting Off the Honey

In order to be a consistent winner, a team must have some cheap baskets. We make every effort to deny the opposition cheap baskets, which we call "honey." There is no doubt that use of zone presses will provide the opponent with some "honey" points, but it is wise not to let a few of them discourage the use of the presses.

The well-drilled ball club will try to make the pressing team pay for running calculated risks. The opposition will try to go to

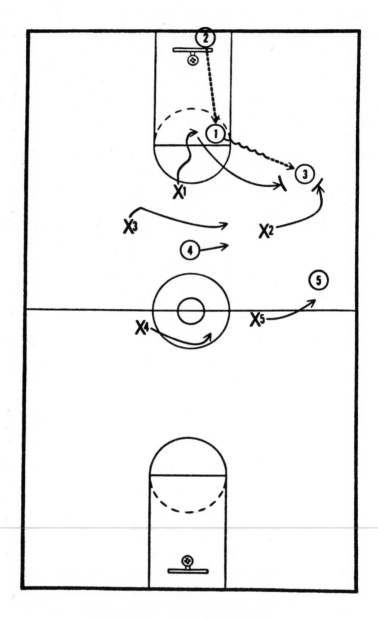

Diagram 7-8. *The 1-2-2 zone press.*

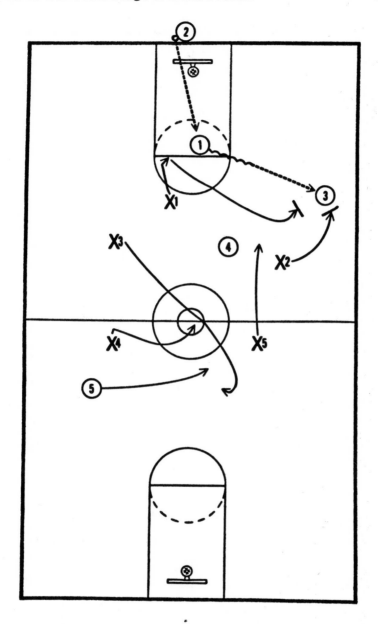

Diagram 7-9. *The 1-2-2 zone press (continued).*

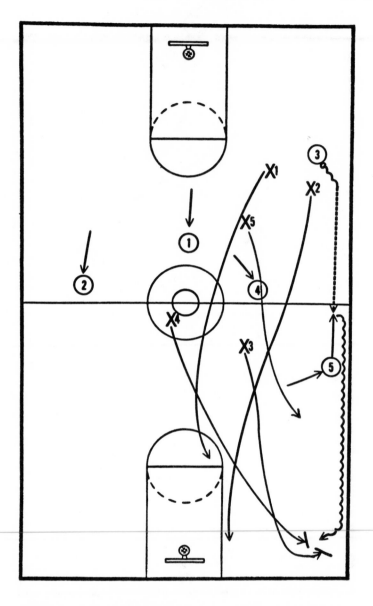

Diagram 7–10. *The 1-2-2 zone press. (Shutting off the honey.)*

the basket once they break a trap, and they will do so with haste. And, as noted, if they have talent and are well drilled, they will come up with occasional easy baskets. Responsive planning simply means we must weigh our turnovers against their cheap baskets. This is the simple decision needed, but it must be made by comparing actual points scored by the pressing team with the cheap baskets by the opponent. Sometimes an analysis made under emotional scenery lulls the pressing team into being satisfied with the turnovers. At times, they may ignore what it is that is done after possession is gained. Offensive planning must be a complement to the use of pressing defenses.

Shutting off the "honey" is shown in Diagram 7–10. X2, the outside man in the trap on O3, comes down the lane on the strong side. X1 hurries down the middle of the lane. They are our smaller and fastest people. X1 and X2 must front offensive people in the lane area who are looking for the ball from O5. Since O5 will often have the seconds necessary to pass before X4 closes the trap, X1 and X2 often come up with turnovers. If we get good action from those covering the lane area, we are happy that O5 can move the ball toward them before X4 can close the trap. Finally, if we get the defensive action we want, it is likely that any shot attempted will be taken under hurried conditions.

We run the "shutting off the honey" drill in practice under scrimmage conditions. Whenever necessary, the action is stopped and then repeated, again and again, from the trap situation at mid-court.

The 2-2-1 Zone Press

The alignment of this defense and movement from it, allows us to have a big man in the basket area and two faster men in action on the front line. Use of the defense is usually dependent upon opposing personnel. It has helped us against ball clubs with one big man on their back line. It also provides better defensive action against teams with talented guards. Movement into traps is easier when executed from the 2-2-1. Point action is still necessary up front. Diagram 7–11 shows the alignment. If the offense brings the ball up in the middle, a guard must overplay it to the side of the dominant arm of the man in possession. Respect must

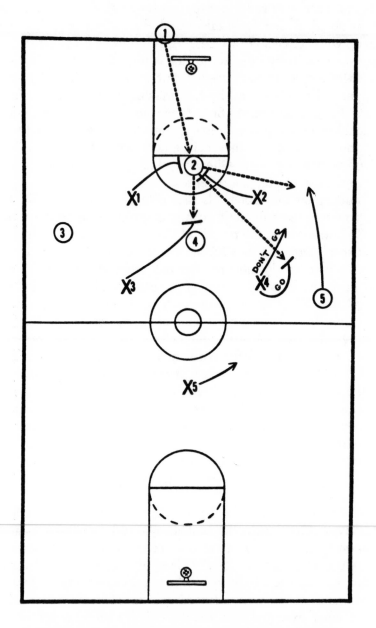

Diagram 7-11. *The 2-2-1 zone press. (Point defense.)*

be given to the harm that the long baseball pass can do; therefore, all players must be keying on the position of the feet of the man in possession. The point man does everything he can to prevent the man with the ball from taking the football passer's stance.

A pass to O4 will be covered by X3. X2 approaches O2 in a route which takes him into the line of vision of O4 and possibly O2. This movement makes daylight for the pass from O2 to O5. X4 will cheat a bit and go for that pass. If O5 moves back far enough toward the ball (as also shown), X4 will not go for it.

If, as in Diagram 7–12, O2 passes to O1, who has come up the sideline, X3 must backtrack and try to get even with O3. If he can, it permits X5 to have some freedom of adjustment. If O3 insists on deep penetration, X5 must start to give him some thought. In such case, X3 contains the sideline movement of O1. X1 turns his back to O1 and trails the play while trying to get the trap in fox hunting style. X2 hustles back to back up the play and X4 does the same. If penetration continues into the corner, the same action is taken by having X1 and X2 hustling to shut off the "honey" play. Corner trapping is executed as in the 1-2-2 zone press.

If, as in Diagram 7–13, the pass does go to the middle, to O4, X3 goes for the ball. And he must go all-out. X4 reacts to X3's move by going into tandem alignment with him. X4 will be ready to contain the ball should it come back to O5 as in the diagram. If the ball comes back, we try to trap by having the man closest to the ball in the first trap (X2) peeling off and giving his back to O5 (fox hunting style), and swinging in a small arc away from him, only to return when and if O3 is brought back by X4. As this occurs, X3 hustles to a tandem alignment with X5 and X1 goes to the head of the circle. Diagram 7–14 shows our alignment now.

If the ball is brought up successfully, we align in a 1-2-2 zone in front of the basket just as we do from whatever defense we use up the floor. We cannot have any confusion as we go into the 1-2-2 zone alignment in the basket area. It's for this reason we go into the same defensive alignment from all our presses. Players have to fill slots coming from the 2-2-1, the 1-2-2 and the 3-2 zone presses. Although this is true, we will often make other defensive changes from that base alignment. Sometimes we play man-to-

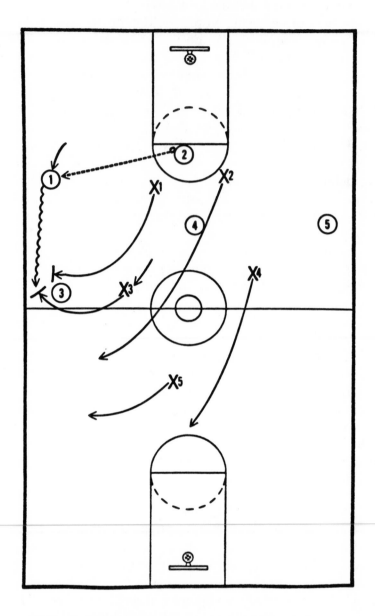

Diagram 7–12. *The 2-2-1 zone press. (Point defense.)*

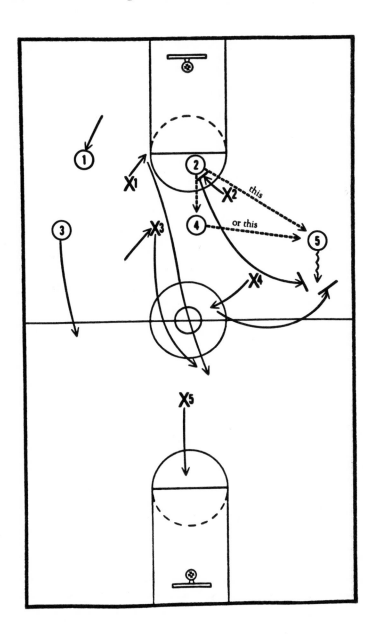

Diagram 7–13. *The 2-2-1 zone press. (Ball coming back.)*

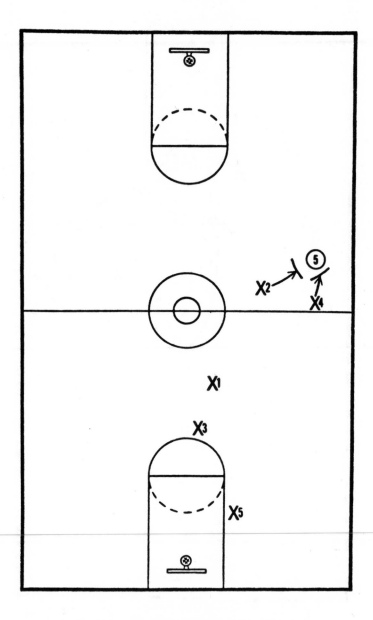

Diagram 7–14. *The 2-2-1 zone press. (Adjustment toward the basket.)*

man against any penetration. At other times, we play man-to-man only on penetration of the ball. Often we are able to play man-to-man while the opposition tries to operate against a zone defense. It seems we often have at least a few seconds before they move people through or overload the defense, which forces us to show our hand.

The 1-2-2 Traditional but Trapping Zone

We trap in this defense only in two areas—the corners and the post. Diagrams 7–15 and 7–16 show the alignment and first movement. The offense is in a typical overload situation which is used against the defense very often. X1 exerts man-to-man play on O1. X2 cheats toward O2 as O1 closes the distance between the two. With the pass by O1 to O2, X1 drops off to the free throw line area. If O2 passes to O5, X2 is ready to go into action. As O2 passes to O5, X2 wheels and storms O5. At the same time, X4 has moved along the base line to close a trap on O5. X5 must front O3 or any man in the middle. Diagram 7–17 shows the progression of movement and X1 going for the ball. From the corner, the ball is almost certain to be passed to O2 or O1. Experience has shown us that X1 operates best if he is given the freedom to go for the ball in either case. He is the only one who will make the decision as the ball comes out of the corner. He is, of course, our fastest player and probably best equipped to succeed in that difficult pass-coverage situation. If O4 goes to the base line, X3 will play him man-to-man. The only opponent left to do effective shooting is O1; he will have defensive action to contend with and he is a good distance from the basket. If O4 stays on the weak side, we are betting they can't get the ball to him.

Trapping the middle poses greater problems, but we still try to do so. Whenever the ball is moved to O2 or O4 (Diagram 7–18), X1 will front O3 as long as he is in the lane area. If O3 goes to a low post position, he must be fronted by either X4 or X5. In the diagram, O4 has passed to O3. In this case, X5 will double-team O3 with X1. X3 will cover any corner threat and X2 sags into the lane. X4 tries to move toward the lane if O5 will permit it, but the former's first responsibility is anyone in the

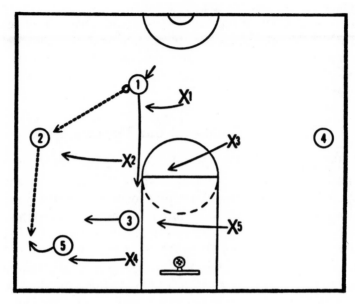

Diagram 7-15. *The 1-2-2 traditional but trapping zone.*

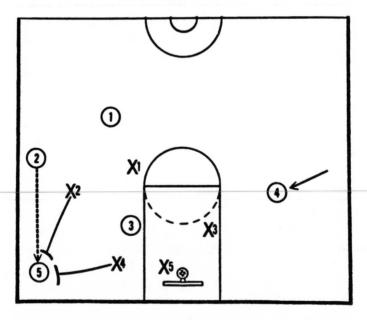

Diagram 7-16. *The 1-2-2 traditional but trapping zone.*

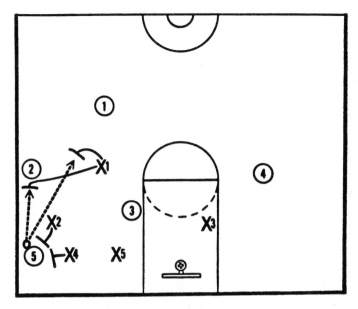

Diagram 7–17. *The 1-2-2 traditional but trapping zone.*

weakside base line area. We don't care where O3 passes the ball, as long as it is moved away from the basket. We don't have turnover plans but merely employ tough defense on the ball and the tactic of forcing them to start again. When they start again, we may be in a different defense.

The One-Half Diamond–Two Defense

This defense is effective against teams which:

1. Play patterned offensive ball and have guards who drive effectively as well as shoot long.
2. Do not have better-than-average shooting ability from the corners.

The defense calls for man-to-man action by the guards and zone execution by the bigger people in the half diamond. And the guards play their men all over with the man-to-man coverage. The basic alignment and beginning movement is shown in Diagram 7–19. We usually place our best rebounder in either the X4

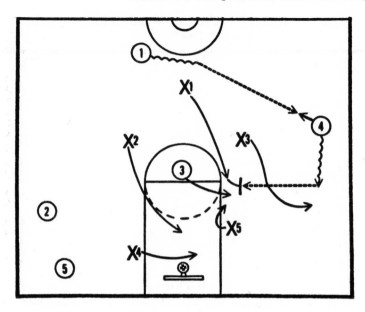

Diagram 7–18. *The 1-2-2 traditional but trapping zone.*

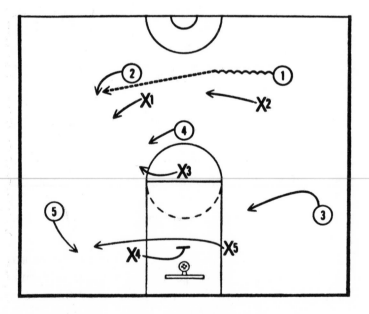

Diagram 7–19. *The one-half diamond–two defense.*

or X5 slot. These men will change, however, from one deep slot to the other whenever action on the ball permits it without risk. If, for example, O1 is dribbling the ball toward mid-court and X2 plays him aggressively, X5, our better rebounder, will start across the lane. The guards must be drilled so as not to allow quick change of direction in the dribble. O2, as he moves away from the ball, becomes a likely receiver. In the diagram, O2 receives the pass and X5 will go across the lane. X4 fills the slot left by X5. Since the opposition has good guards and since we play them man-to-man, the guards will often dribble enough to allow us to make the movement safely. *But again, the defensive guards must prevent a quick change of direction in the dribble.* The deep switch helps if a pass is made to O5 because X5 is in motion and better able to cover O5. In that case, X4 would stop on the ball side of the basket.

Diagram 7–20 depicts an offensive situation which has become an overload. When this happens, the players in the half diamond are drilled to play man-to-man within the zone part of the defense. X5 has defensive shape on O5. X3, X4 and X5 must be disciplined as to how far out they will go. We vary such instruction to them, depending on the shooting ability of the opponent in those areas. *We will not use this defense if their bigger people shoot the 12- to 15-footer with accuracy.* If two of their big men shoot well at that distance, *we may use it.* And if only one has good shooting ability at the same distance, *we certainly will use it.* It follows, of course, that if all three have shooting troubles at such distances, *we would use this defense.*

If a guard penetrates on a dribble, we try to give him tough defense by having our guard play him up to the line indicated in Diagram 7–20. Line A   B is approximately that line. As O2 nears the line, X3 will engage him. X1 exerts the necessary pressure to deny the jump shot by O2. As X3 challenges the ball, X1 slacks off. Now X1 must make a decision which only he can make. He may thwart a possible pass to O4 or he may trap the ball with X3. Usually there is ample defensive pressure to handle O2, and X1 helps most by becoming involved with O4. But we still want the decision to be made by X1. He will continue to play on O2 if O2 moves to other areas of the floor. If O1 remains where he is or moves toward the middle, X2 will drop off to the head of the

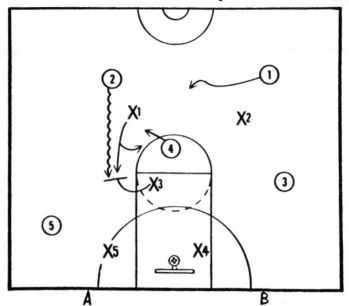

Diagram 7-20. *The one-half diamond–two defense.*

circle. He still keeps man-to-man responsibility on O2 wherever the latter goes.

The defense calls for some definite guidelines which help players execute their moves without thinking. (You can't play defense and think at the same time.) In Diagram 7–21, O5 again moves into an overload situation not involving guards and this requires an adjustment. Our guideline in this case is: "You must leave your area of the zone if there is no one in it, and if overloading takes place elsewhere from the free throw line and that line extended to the base line." If, as in the diagram, the ball is passed from O2 to O1, X1 drops to the head of the circle. Again, however, X1 will go with O2 wherever he goes. The ideal defensive situation would be one in which O2 remains in the area shown. As O5 goes over the base line, X5 tightens up on O3 as the ball reaches O1. X4 will now cross the lane, but he does not try to give O5 tight coverage. The determination of applying tight coverage on O5 or not will depend on the latter's shooting ability from the corner and how far he goes to the corner. If the ball is passed to O5 and we do not respect his shooting, X4 will remain about as shown. X3 and X1 (if in that area) must prevent

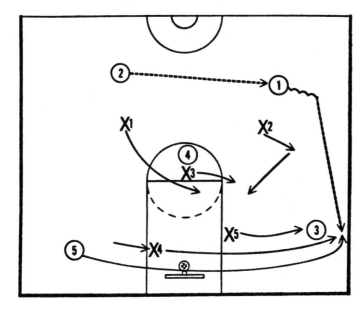

Diagram 7–21. *The one-half diamond–two defense.*

any "back door" play by either O4 or O2. As soon as O1 passes to O5, X2 drops off.

This defense has helped us immeasurably. I prefer to use it only in the second half. It isn't an easy defense to smell out, and I'd rather not allow the opponent a half-time session in which to make the adjustments.

Frankly, our league consists of teams ranging from big men of good shooting ability to no "good shooting" big men. There are very few with three good-shooting big men. We do have an abundance of very good guards who shoot and move very well. The one-half diamond–two defense is tailored then to do well against many teams in our league. This may not be your case, of course, but I really feel all levels of play have few teams which include three big men who are good shooters. We have had nights when the opposition would drive their guards repeatedly and run into the zone part of the defense. There they experienced shooting trouble, offensive fouls and bad passing conditions.

The defense does quite well against the original "shuffle" and some of the variations thereto. As a player I was taught the shuffle by the master, Bruce Drake, at the University of Oklahoma. I recall thinking then about the weakside force-pass situation—if that pass were defensed tough, the offense might not get started. In addition, if that pass is completed, teams are so interested in executing that great offense that they pay little heed to the meaning of the situation wherein there is no defense on the man receiving the force pass. The zone part of the defense can come up quick enough to give that man shooting problems; therefore, the players in the one-half diamond zone can cause any patterned offense a real headache.

Diagram 7–22 relates to the situation. In the diagram, X3 exerts good pressure on O3 and denial of the ball. Diagram 7–23 shows X3 allowing O3 to receive the ball uncontested. In either case, the one-half diamond–two defense can remain intact, action of X3 notwithstanding. I think I know what Bruce Drake would do in either of these cases, but others may not be aware of just what they would do.

Sometimes I think the chief benefit of concocting an offense is in developing a sharp awareness of how it can best be defensed. If you get other clubs to use your offense, you should be

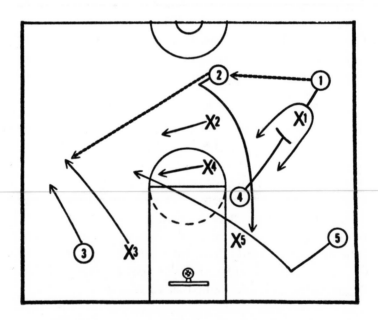

Diagram 7–22. *The one-half diamond–two defense.*

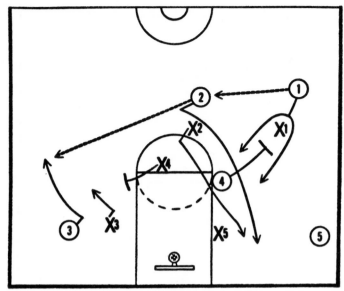

Diagram 7-23. *The one-half diamond–two defense.*

in great shape to defense it. Maybe that is why there is little to fear in writing a book about any phase of the game.

If the offense overloads any part of the defense, we cover the overloaded part with man-to-man action if the position of the ball permits it. Diagram 7-24 shows the offense in such alignment: O3 and O4 are overloading. As long as O1 has the ball, we will stay as shown. But as the ball is passed to O2, we will cover with X3 on O3 and X4 on O4. If O3 moves toward the sideline, the man-to-man play would continue. X5 goes to the lane and X1 will drop to the circle, unless O1 moves out of the area. In this case we still have the diamond alignment, but some of the zone people will go man-to-man and the defensive guard fills the zone if the offensive guards let him.

Since the offensive guards do put the ball to the floor a great deal, we plan traps for that movement. We like those guards to cross paths. We don't try to trap a big man underneath with two big men. If, for example, in Diagram 7-25, O2 dribbles as shown, we will attack him with X2 trying to close the trap. Our bigger man, near the base line, will not go for the trap. X1 tries to go to the circle and X5 tightens to the lane. There are times when the ball will get to O3 and we want X5 or X3 to assume a helper role.

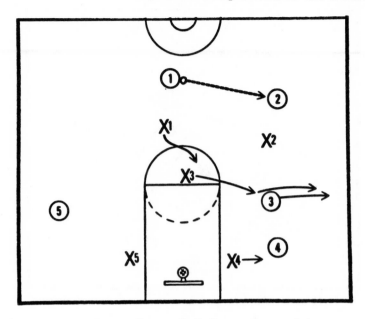

Diagram 7–24. *The one-half diamond–two defense.*

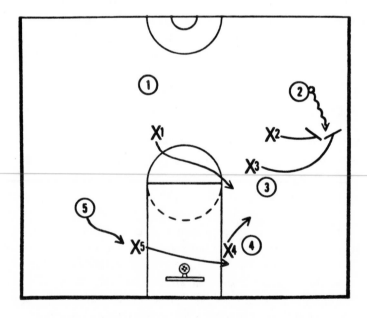

Diagram 7–25. *The one-half diamond–two defense.*

The men in the one-half diamond zone are drilled to trap in the corners with a guard.

The 3-2 Mid-Court Zone Press

Operating this press still requires point action by the middle man in the three line. Although he doesn't step out as far as he does in the "point" or "flat" defenses, we feel an early indication of ball movement toward one sideline or the other is a help to us. We use two bigger men in the back line. Diagram 7-26 shows the alignment and start of movement. We like to have a sideline indication on ball movement about in the area of X2. The back line men try to align in such a way as to get a straight line with anyone in back of them and the ball. As X2 turns O2, X3 contains

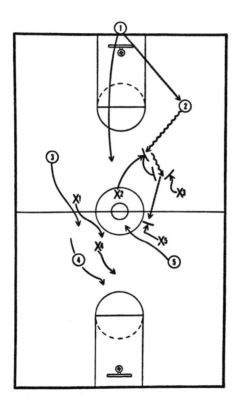

Diagram 7-26. *The 3-2 mid-court zone press.*

and X2 and X3 go for the trap. Now we want man-to-man action on anyone moving to the middle of the zone. Often O4 or O5 will try to "post" the zone. Either X4 or X5 prevents that pass to the middle. If O3 goes to the middle spot, then X1 shuts off the pass. If O3 causes no problem in the middle, we have X4 slide to the right and X1 backs up the middle. Action continues in Diagram 7–27. If O5 moves to the sideline, it becomes X4's task to contain him. If a pass is made to O5, X3 will leave the first trap with his back to O5, and try to get into the second trap with X4 if O5 can be halted, or, better still, brought back a step or two. X2 now hustles to the point position of the 1-2-2 zone, X1 is ready to assume one spot in the same defense and X5 will go to the deep alignment on the strong side. The result is seen in Diagram 7–28. And in Diagram 7–29, the 1-2-2 zone, our basic defensive alignment in front of the basket, has been organized.

Diagram 7–27. *The 3-2 mid-court zone press.*

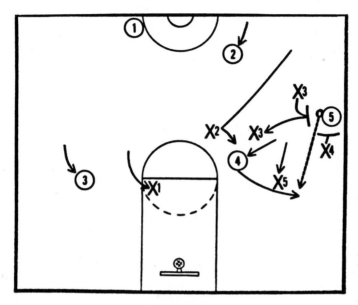

Diagram 7–28. *The 3-2 mid-court zone press.*

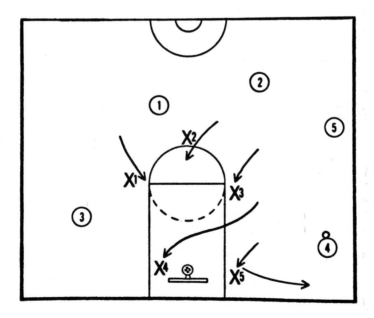

Diagram 7–29. *The 3-2 mid-court zone press.*

Getting Possession and Controlling Tempo in the Destroyer Offense

8 • • • • • • • •

How to Drill for
Effective Rebounding

A good big man will usually beat a good
little man in the rebounding game, but there are methods of
execution which can make this less often the case. Sound planning
and excellent execution can make the situation more equitable.
Our rebounding efforts are given a shot in the arm by an innovation which can help to improve any team's rebounding ability. If
you enjoy efficient defensive rebounding execution the innovation
may not be helpful to you, but we have found it to be very helpful every year.

In some drills and scrimmages, the offensive team is allowed
to go get the ball after they have scored. *Yes, this means a team
has the right to score 4, 6 or 8 points by getting the ball after it
clears the net. They may shoot again and again, but at no time
may they touch the net.*

For practice sessions, then, we change the rule of the game
which gives possession of the ball to the opposing team after the
offensive team scores. This puts a tremendous amount of importance on defensive rebounding. Using the rule innovation helps
demonstrate the importance of blocking out and facilitates the execution of particular moves with certainty; if not, the defense suf-
fers by staying on defense. And that's where I want them until

they learn the importance and technique of blocking out on the defensive boards. They need more opportunities to develop better defensive rebounding, and we will provide those opportunities. The innovation doesn't necessarily teach "how" to block out, but it impresses players with the absolute necessity of learning. Again, if the defensive rebounder doesn't get the ball, he knows the opposition will be allowed to score again and again, if they can get the ball from the net after scoring. The "how" of blocking out is taught and drilled in various ways.

Undoubtedly some coaches will react to this change of rules for practice sessions by saying, "Are you kidding? It's a free-for-all under the boards now. It might ruin some of my ball players for the rebounding game."

Well, we look at it differently. First, if we don't block out in the defensive rebound situation, we want those players guilty of not doing so to be penalized. And a very effective way to do so is to have the score affect the guilty negatively. They must conquer their inability or unwillingness to do the job. Secondly, defensive blocking out and offensive rebounding are two of the most difficult phases of the game to teach. Most of us say, or intimate at least, that height and aggressiveness are what is needed to develop good rebounders. Then we drill particular methods of doing so and holler our heads off for correct execution *as the action is taking place,* or what is worse, *after the action has taken place.* I am not interested in wasting time on spilled milk. The ideal teaching method would include a penalty; a penalty built into the action, as it is happening. Players will usually suffer that penalty once or twice, but no more, if they practice under the rule change I am suggesting.

If a shooter gets possession after the ball clears the net, what must he do to shoot again? Most often he will take a step away from the basket and jump. This gives the defensive man time and room to get inside shape. If he doesn't, he should suffer the strongest penalty we can devise. *No more than two successive baskets should ever occur.*

The Rule Innovation for Practice and the Big Man

Perhaps your next concern will be for the supposed advantage of the big man under the boards. Let's explore your concern. Who has the physical advantage after the ball clears the net—the 6-foot, 10-inch boy, the 7-footer or the smaller player? The rim is at a height of 10 feet. Although I haven't measured the net (it hasn't been necessary to do so in order to realize the innovation is successful), I know it extends down at least 14 inches. That places the bottom of the net at a height of 8 feet, 10 inches. The 6-footer can extend either or both arms, in almost all cases, a distance of 2 feet. This places the ball almost in front of the 6-footer, with no jump at all.

Now the big man will have to reach down toward the net to gain possession. This is a definite disadvantage, since he is quite apt to touch the net; therefore, the 6-footer enjoys an advantage over the 7-footer as the ball clears the net.

The Jump Shot

What percentage of all shots taken today are jump shots? The percentage is very high. And while that shooter is jumping to deliver the ball, the defensive man has no excuse for not getting inside shape.

I'll admit there is a small war (and rather often a big war) now under the boards if the defensive man gets the rebound shape he should have. In the case of the jump shooter, he at least is out of the rebound action if the defensive man executes satisfactorily. So, in the case of the jump shooter trying to get position while in the air, he is met with an impossibility. In that case then, the small war becomes no war, and most of the big wars would become small ones.

The Lay-Up

What about the lay-up? As the shooter turns the ball loose, he certainly is not in a situation from which he can get shape for ensuing action quickly. If the defensive man doesn't keep him out of that action, we want the offensive man to have the right to get the ball and score again.

The One-Hand Push Shot

The shooting situation which causes the most problems in blocking out execution on the shooter is involved with the push shot or the outdated "set shot." The shooter has his feet on the floor as the shot is taken, and he can go into rebound action immediately. If players are well drilled with regard to this rule in practice sessions, they will contain that shooter too.

Post Man Shooting

Any shot by a post man is taken without the shooter using much speed or momentum. Quickness is the name of the game for the post man's shot, but momentum and speed toward the basket are usually not important factors. However, the post man is ready to go to the board quickly. If he is not blocked out, you are in trouble. If you allow him to get his own rebound, or possession after he scores, the defense quickly appreciates the necessity of keeping him out of there. Again, you don't have to shout, threaten or cajole. After the post man gets two successive baskets on one or two occasions, the defensive man automatically gets involved satisfactorily.

Defensing the Out-Of-Bounds Play

The man passing the ball from out of bounds often becomes the shooter. If the defensive man relaxes mentally, he may allow his opponent to get a shot uncontested. Since it is uncontested, this means the shooter often has a clear path to the basket and a second basket. If you use our rule, with this rule variation, it will happen only once. That defensive man has had the results of his mental error indelibly branded in his mind. You don't believe it? Try it!

The Trailer Play in the Fast Break

So many times a trailer is the man getting 2 points because his defensive man commits a mental error and as a result doesn't hustle to get involved. If that trailer goes to the basket "clean," he will also have a second basket on most occasions, if the rule mentioned is used. *That mental error infuriates me.* Oftentimes, a big man doesn't hustle to handle the trailer. If the trailer converts for 4 points, the defensive man is immediately and acutely aware he cannot afford such mental laziness. Again, all the shouting in practice is no longer necessary in games. You don't believe it? Try it!

Team Rebounding

Of course four other players other than the shooter must be included in the defensive rebounding department. Concern for the shooter is just one-fifth of the problem. Nevertheless, we have found that if our other man-to-man rules are carried out, the defensive men, off the ball, are less prone to let their opponents penetrate. It may be that most teams are drilled to have the shooter go for the rebound, and perhaps that shooter knows better than anyone else where the ball is falling.

The real problem that must be dealt with is that of watching the ball in the few seconds after a shot is taken. If the defense commits that error, our rule affords the offense an excellent opportunity for more than just 2 points.

The mental error of watching the ball after a shot is understandable. Most of us teach players to be ball conscious in almost all other phases of the game. Many defenses today are predicated on being more ball conscious than ever before. The shout often heard is, "see the ball" or "watch for the ball." And then, in the rebounding game, we insist that the defense may not watch the ball after a shot is taken so that better floor position can be gained. The two cases are contradictory. *When two contradictory mental processes call for two contradictory physical actions, some strong mental discipline is necessary to handle those contradictions.* I don't believe this mental discipline is very easy to develop during the average rebound drilling sessions characterizing the practices of many teams. We believe our rule change for practice sessions does the job easily and simply, without much ado.

The Rule Change and Fouling

In practice sessions, if a shooter is fouled as he delivers the shot, we ignore the infraction unless the shot is missed. If the offensive team is fouled *after* or *as* the ball is being taken from the net, the foul is respected; therefore, a 5-point play is possible. You may say more points are possible too, but it just doesn't happen.

So, our explanation to our players is, "If the offensive team scores either a field goal or a free throw, any of its members will be allowed to take the ball from the net, without touching the latter, and score a second successive basket if they are able. They may shoot again and again. You must get inside shape and keep the offense as far from the basket as possible. You must block out to achieve that objective. No one may touch the net—and, obviously, no one will be given possession out of bounds automatically because his opponent scores."

Weird? Revolutionary? Absurd? Try it before you condemn it or condone it.

Finally, the only problem we have found in using the rule change is in getting the squad to believe what is going to happen. It takes them a short while to accept our explanations. Although we explain and demonstrate the change, players just do not react to the rule favorably in the first few sorties. As already indicated, however, it is a very temporary disbelief. No one can relish seeing 2 points become 4 or 5 in the same few seconds. This, then, points to the mental problem of developing good defensive rebounding. The rebounders are optimistic that they will get the ball. The weak defender in the rebound situation is weak because he unconsciously feels his ball club will get possession, no matter what he does or doesn't do. And that's what we often teach, either by spelling it out or intimating it—we get the biggest guys we can in a few positions and tell them to get the ball for us. That tends to develop poor rebounding on the part of the smaller people, who are so many more in numbers. The rule change challenges big and little man alike, *as the action is happening.*

A Sequel to the Practice Rule Change

A sequel to the rule change and its effect on defensive rebounding is that the offensive rebounding becomes vicious as the offensive team adapts to the right to shoot again right after converting. There is no need to elaborate on it. It is obvious that the offense is given great incentive to go get the ball. This causes the defensive board work to be more devastating. And a cycle is struck between the two. We have never had a boy over 6 feet, 6 inches, and yet we have won two Northern Division Championships of the New England State College Athletic Conference in six years. Winning or losing in large part is decided on the backboards.

Frankly, I don't like to penalize perfection. And sometimes I have considered the rule change described as an appropriate one for the accepted rules of the game. Why should the player who meets the objective of the game be forced to give up the ball because he succeeds? On the other hand, perhaps being the only one (to my knowledge) using the rule may be a decided advantage.

Defensive Rebounding Drills

Of course we try to teach the mechanics of rebounding in certain ways. We don't just rely on mental attitudes to get the ball, even though those attitudes are as important as they are. I don't know if the way we do it is unique or not but it gets the job done.

Our principal defensive rebounding drill is done "by the numbers," in military fashion. The drill is started the first day of the second week of practice, which is usually the third week in October. During that first week, each player's defensive rebounding execution is checked very carefully. Some need more emphasis than others. Taking up too much time at this point is bad. I am constantly fearful of wasting time with players who do a commendable job, possibly hurting them in the process mentally. The execution checked is that movement done by the numbers. We aren't interested in the complete, fluid blocking-out movement in that first week.

The stance is taught first. Six players are spread out at each end of the floor. No opposition is used. The outside leg is back. A coach hollers "shot" (no one is actually shooting), and each player does what amounts to an about-face *without turning his head*. The toes of the outside foot are raised, and the heel of the inside foot as well. As the body is turned, the eyes remain steadfast to the front. This is repeated until all players make the turn six times, without any one of them turning his head as the body is turned. Six repetitions without error are required each time the drill is used.

Then the coach shouts "one," and the players bring the rear leg (inside leg) to a position level with the outside leg. That rear leg must be brought toward the other leg so that the distance between feet is approximately 2 feet at the end of the movement. This gives a square, crouching and low-center-of-gravity position. This phase of the drill is also executed six times without error. We have not done so yet but we are going to call this our "66 drill"—six players, six times . . . perfectly.

When the coach shouts "two," the players start to move slowly toward the basket and bring their eyes to a forward-looking position *as they do so.*

Finally, each rebounder goes for a ball, which we drop somewhere in front of the backboard. (Six balls are dropped, one for each man in the drill.)

Preferably we would have the offensive rebounders on the hips of our defensive rebounders, but if the drill described is executed correctly we don't worry if that is not the case. The man recovering the ball must shout "ball" in a clear, sharp voice when he gains possession. This is vital if we want to go into a fast break. Other than that it is just good policy to let all our people know we have possession, as soon as possible. I feel pressure defenses are sometimes more vulnerable to attack by that good, quick call of "ball." Things often get done before the opposition can organize their defense. And this doesn't mean a fast break is always used to do so. For example, if a pressure defense is expected, we are able to organize the "Destroyer Offense" readily.

The offensive rebounder many times will take a step or two in one direction or another in an effort to fake the defensive man. In this case, contact probably will not take place. If the fake step(s) is taken, it means the offense will have to take additional steps to go directly toward the ball finally. During the seconds used to do so, the ball usually falls to the floor or is bouncing on the floor. The faking step(s) is concerned with the positions of our rebounders, but not with the interval of time in which the ball falls. And both must be considered. The name of the game in rebounding is one step, two steps; 1 second, 2 seconds; etc.

The defensive rebounder takes his eyes off the offensive man when the latter *starts movement* toward the board. He must move in the "squared" position and *try to penetrate as slowly as his opponent will permit.* A line is sometimes taped on the floor about 3 feet from the basket in a semi-circle. This is used as a limit beyond which the rebounder must not go. Players must be drilled, of course, not to be taken too far under the boards, which would make them ineffective rebounders.

The Defensive Rebounding Drill with Opposition

We now use the drill with opposition. And, as indicated, we drill from a man-to-man alignment with no thought of coming from a zone alignment. Even when using zones we will adjust in different ways, trying to rebound in a man-to-man effort. The offensive men may do whatever they please, but they must shoot within 5 seconds. As the shot is taken, the defensive man involved must holler "shot." It is very important that he make that call and we are very upset if it is not done. Both ends of the floor are used until each player has been in the limelight long enough to be checked for execution.

The drill is then executed in a 3-on-3 situation. Again, the shout of "ball" must be heard when possession is gained, as well as "shot" whenever the opposition makes a shooting effort. In September or during other out-of-season times when our players are enjoying an impromptu game among themselves, they do make those calls. This is proof the calls are made automatically and without conscious effort.

At least with some teams, it is probably important that the coach or other people don't do some of the players' talking. It is possible for this to happen, which tends to detract from important player talk during the ball games.

The 5-on-5 Rebounding Drill

As mentioned, at times we want to move into the fast break from the defensive boards. In fact, it is good policy always to try to do so if the opposition is susceptible. This being the case, our

defensive rebounding drills include a variation which helps in the
beginning stages of the break. One and the same guard is designated as the first outlet pass receiver, every time. If the guards
are playing against opposition which doesn't become involved
with the rebound action, we will have the first outlet pass area
filled and the second guard (same guard every time) filling the
second outlet pass area—the middle. This is shown in Diagram
8–1. It is intended that one of the bigger men will beat his man,
which would give us a 3-on-2 break. If the opposing guards do
not try to rebound, we have to assume they will be in defensive
alignment from which they can cope with just a two-man break.
Therefore, it is wise to plan to beat them by getting one of our
bigger men into the early break alignment. And we try to ready
ourselves for this contingency as a part of our game plan every
game. An opposing big man is picked out who we feel would be
most susceptible to such tactics. Completion of the drill is reached
when the ball is in the middle of the floor and one of the big men
is in or near that area. Five men repeat the drill until execution
is satisfactory five times.

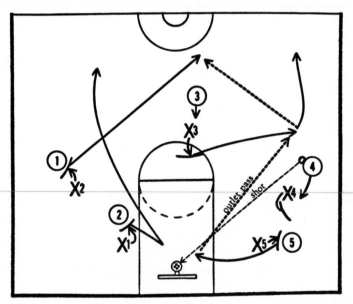

Diagram 8–1. *The fast break from the defensive re-*
bounding drill.

The "Tiger Drill"

A second drill used to help develop quickness and peripheral vision, so important in rebounding, is the "tiger drill." I'm not so sure it helps defensive rebounding any more than it does offensive rebounding, but I do know it helps both to some degree. Among other things, it provides rebound action with ample body contact.

Diagram 8–2 illustrates the drill. X1, X2 and X3 are positioned as shown. The coach under the basket will put the ball(s) in play. One manager is placed on each side of the floor to act as a retriever. X1, X2 and X3 *face the other basket.* The coach will roll the ball in any direction, throw it so as to cause bouncing movement or hurl it into the air. When the coach shouts "go," the rebounders turn as quickly as possible and locate the ball. They all go for it, and one of them gains possession, taking the good shot. The two men not gaining possession play defense immediately, 2-on-1. And they must block out defensively, as has been explained. If the shooter converts, he may get the ball from the net and score again. No swinging of the arms is allowed

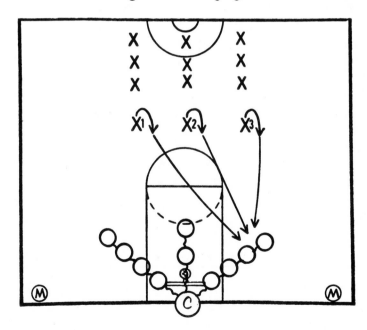

Diagram 8–2. *The "tiger drill."*

unless the elbows are flexed. And we want the two defenders to hang all over the man with the ball *before the shot and the rebounding action.* After the shot, we want nothing but the best defensive rebounding action possible. And *each defensive rebounder must battle the other in trying to be the one who blocks the shooter.* If the shooter gets the rebound or the ball from the net, I am *extremely* unhappy with the other two.

The man who gains possession may double dribble without penalty, but *he must move toward the basket. He may not take a single step in any direction away from the basket.* No fouls are called. Two balls can be used in the drill, and therefore one player will not gain possession. That player then must try to stop one offensive man from scoring. If he can somehow stop both he will have done an outstanding defensive job, which helps to redeem himself for not having gained possession. You will find trying to defense both men calls for some defensive scooting. On occasion that man has been able to stop both shooters. If he tries to stop both and then stops neither, we are again very unhappy.

The drill also aids in building better ball movement, of course, simply because it helps us get possession more often. And again, the best way to learn to play is by executing moves under game conditions. If we can increase the number of times we gain possession and then the length of time we run our patterns, we have more opportunities to learn to play the game better.

A variation of the drill includes using a fourth man. He is in the X4 slot. The man in that slot may not go for the ball, but he becomes the second offensive man once possession is gained. Then the drill is run as a 2-on-2 situation. Quick movement is developed if the coach shouts "go" after the ball has been allowed to roll very close to the players. The development of peripheral vision is helped if he shouts "go" after the ball is thrown high in the air. Quick head movement is also required in such cases.

The Head-to-Head Defensive Rebounding Drill

I feel this is a very necessary drill. It is used with some variation by most coaches and comes as nothing new from my mind, but I must include it because of one little wrinkle we add. That wrinkle probably is unique.

Diagram 8–3 illustrates the drill and the footwork. Two players face the basket on the free throw line. A ball is tossed off the board and players go for it. This is really an offensive drill then, except that the way we designate one player to go for the ball is a defensive maneuver, as we think of it. The man designated tries to put his inside foot in front of his opponent's. A small but important detail must be executed in order to gain that inside position. *Each player is taught not to move the inside foot in a lateral direction first, but rather forward and then laterally.* If he gains the inside position, the player will then swing his other leg to place himself with his back to the basket. He must then welcome contact on the chest with either both of his hands over his head or hanging at his side. We don't want the hands held at mid-body position which invites a holding foul. The rebounder must take whatever jolt the other player gives him. Therefore the drill is essentially a defensive drill. We don't care where the ball goes as long as the opposition is held in outside shape. This type of action is appropriate for the occasions when the defense can't get in front

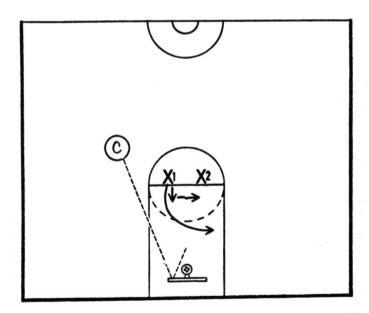

Diagram 8–3. *Getting inside shape on the rebound drill.*

of the offensive man but defensive blocking out is still mandatory.

The footwork shown in the diagram is as follows: the short arrow of X1 moving toward the basket is the inside foot and the longer arrow shows the lateral movement of the same leg. The longest, unbroken arrow is the outside foot going into position.

Rebounding from the Defensive Free Throw Alignment

Actually the same movement used in the head-to-head drill is used when the opposition shoots free throws, except for the man who will cut off the shooter. Diagram 8–4 shows the situation. X1, X2, X3 and X4 step forward with their inside feet as quickly as possible, and then the feet are moved laterally toward the opponent. *We don't allow the inside foot to move laterally toward the opponent.* Of course the movement differs from that of Diagram 8–3, in that we don't swing the outside leg since we already have closer proximity to the basket.

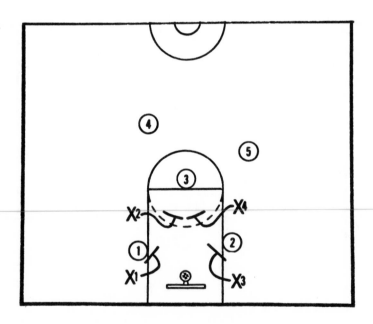

Diagram 8–4. *Defensive free throw alignment and movement.*

The fifth man, X5, is not shown in the diagram, since it is our plan to have him align in the area, enabling him to get involved with the opponent's toughest rebounder if it becomes necessary.

Theory and Reality

Basketball is a non-contact game in theory, and in reality it is a man-handling proposition on the defensive boards where ball games are won or lost. I was once asked in Spain to define basketball. I put it this way, "Basketball is violent dance, wherein your partner is not friendly or loveable but an enemy." We have no sympathy for the player who doesn't relish contact on the defensive boards. *He will not play for us.*

Ten minutes per practice is spent on the drills described after satisfactory execution is reached. Obviously, drill time is considered differently than teaching time. Teaching time to be allocated is determined by achieving execution, while drill time is repeated proof the learning has taken place. The blocking out maneuver must be mastered.

9 · · · · · · · · ·

How to Develop Accurate Free Throw Shooting

A number of years ago, a random sampling of game statistics showed that about 42% of the games reported could have been won on the free throw line. I have never forgotten that report. Although the statistics may change from study to study and from year to year, the importance of the statement calls for utmost consideration of free throw shooting. If 35% conversion from the floor is acceptable shooting, then the figure of 70% from the free throw line seems to be an acceptable figure. I feel the differential result between shooting against opposition and no opposition should be double. Our players know that no one will be allowed *to start a game if he has not converted at least 70% over the previous five ball games*. No one is exempt from this rule. Yes, they are given the first five ball games to establish the percentage and then the percentage is computed so as to omit the first game played, after the sixth game is in the books. This is done throughout the season and allows us to apply the rule for every game in the season after the first five.

There is no doubt the players feel great pressure because of this policy, but I feel the importance of this phase of the game warrants exerting it. And I also feel it helps to cause greater concentration on execution in practice and ball games. We don't *try* to impress players with the importance of *every* free throw, *we do so.* If this isn't achieved, free throw shooting in practice will lack the necessary concentration. Lo and behold, some players tend to belittle the importance of the free throw, even in the early stages of a ball game. If the score is tight in the second half, then the importance of each free throw is obvious and the pressure builds. Unfortunately, the percentage of free throws missed increases as the game continues. If the player doesn't convert satisfactorily in the early stages of the game, what will the situation be as fatigue becomes more of a factor? Of course, there are exceptions. There will always be that exceptional performer who rises to the occasion because he is a super competitor. But the coach must concern himself with an entire organization, and with all players. So, we live by rules which are concerned with the healthy winning attitude of an entire organization. Therefore, I cringe with every missed free throw. I become plain irritated in practice if unsatisfactory results are received at that time. I cringe if we miss a free throw in the first few seconds of a game as we are trying to go ahead 1-0. And I've heard about the superstition of losing if your team scores the first point. But I want to score the first, the last and all possible points in between. A battle is no place for superstitions. A battle is a place for execution of things learned (then drilled as close to perfection as possible) and inspiration. Every player must concentrate on every free throw attempted in practice as well as in ball games. The coach's insistence in practice will help to produce the same effort in the ball game.

Frankly, I believe there are various methods involving body mechanics which will produce successful free throw shooting. But I also believe there are some points which are common to the varying methods.

Body Mechanics in Free Throw Shooting

We believe the shooter should imagine himself standing on top of a skyscraper and leaning over the edge of that structure.

He should look over (conquer the fear) and learn to balance himself so that he never falls off. Thus he is as close to the basket as possible. As the shot is taken he may even touch the line or go over it, but the ball will always make prior contact with the rim, the backboard or enter the basket. Thus a violation is never a problem in our way of approaching free throw shooting. (And at this point, the comparison to the skyscraper ends.)

The least amount of muscular action possible is a desirable achievement in delivering the free throw. We ask the shooter to shoot the free throw as he does any other shot on the floor, without jumping. We don't try to dictate the position of the shooter's hands on the ball. We don't position the feet, except that one foot must take the skyscraper position. The knees must be in a slightly flexed position. The eyes are concentrated on the front part of the rim, and the shooting effort should be to put the ball "just over the rim."

There will be exceptions which should be allowed, but the rule from which we work is that the only movement absolutely necessary is the extension of the knees and the wrist action delivering the ball. The physical power to deliver the shot comes from the body as the knees move from flexion to extension. The wrists trigger the shot. Bringing the ball down toward the belt line with entire arm movement is an error responsible for inaccuracies. Deeper flexion of the knees also causes unnecessary extension. Elimination of the former eliminates the latter.

If there is any secret in the execution of our free throw shooting it exists in the way we run our free throw drills in practice. And this is one phase of practice I do not miss. Everyone is asked to urge everyone else on to greater depths of concentration in shooting free throws. The floor should be heavy with silence during this phase of practice.

The Entire Season's Free Throw Shooting Plan

Desired physical execution decreases as physical fatigue increases. Practice plans for free throw shooting should be made with that thought in mind. The problem is compounded by the psychological processes as well. The release of a player from fierce resistance (shot from the floor) to no resistance(the free throw) changes that player psychologically in some way, to some extent, sometimes. Our plans to develop good free throw shooting are made with that thought in mind too.

Overall we like to "peak" the first part of February (according to our season), which leaves us with the problem of keeping that "peak form" until late February or early March tournament time. On the other hand, we expect the free throw performance to "peak" in the first game and stay that way for the rest of the season.

After two weeks of practice (the end of October), we hope to have all players grooved with their particular delivery of the ball. By "grooving" I mean to have each player consistent in his delivery of the ball. On certain occasions there will be players who are allowed to experiment with a different delivery after that time, but this opportunity is afforded to freshmen and sophomores only. This gives us the month of November to drill the delivery until it is down pat. We learn in October, drill toward perfection in November and execute that 70% minimum conversion in the first ball game of December. Our computation of the percentage is also based on pre-season practice sessions and scrimmages, but the rule does not go into force until five games are played.

Players are informed of the rule early in November. The actual statement made is, "No one will be a starter in a game if his free throw percentage isn't 70% or higher over a five-game span. You are given the first five games to establish your percentage." It is worth repeating that players seem to accept this pressure by applying more effort to their concentration. *No matter what else an individual can do, you aren't going to be a champion without successful free throw shooting.* Many are the cases which can be cited.

The Free Throw Practice Timetable

Although varying adjustments are always necessary from time to time in October, each player takes 25 free throws at the start of practice. As already stated, efforts are now being made to "groove" their delivery. Similar to the golf swings for different clubs, we want the ball delivered with the same motion for this unique shooting effort of basketball. Players, managers and coaches all help each player to concentrate. We keep no locker room chart showing daily achievements, but we do post the percentage achieved on a weekly basis. A manager notes the percentage made each day.

Early in December, players take 15 free throws at the start of practice and ten about halfway through each practice. By December 15th, we take ten at the halfway mark and ten at the end of practice. By the third week in January, we take five shots dispersed over the entire practice. In February I put them on the line at random times, and one, two or three shots are taken at the end of practice. If one is taken and they convert, they are sent to the showers happy; the same thing occurs if the second and third shots are taken. If they miss, however, genuine dissatisfaction is displayed, just as the shooter himself develops the same reaction upon missing in a vital situation.

The preparation of a basketball team, at best, should include efforts to practice under the best simulation of game conditions possible. Players don't go to the line for five, ten or 50 successive free throws in game conditions. They are on the line for an occasional free throw from once to ten or 12 times in a game. Our practice of the free throw is organized then to meet that premise. Since the October and November free throw work is an effort to groove the shot, my thoughts are not contradictory. Grooving the delivery makes it possible for the shooter to go to the line once or twice and shoot successfully, if that is his practice habit.

It is my usual procedure to watch free throw shooting from various places on the floor. This has been very helpful in efforts to point out mistakes being made by the shooter. The side view (about 10 feet away) shows the shooter in profile and helps to "break the shot down" from the standpoint of knees, arms and stance in relation to the line. Standing to the rear of the shooter will show hand and wrist action. A frontal position will allow the coach to make sure the shooter's eyes are on the front rim and not lifting to follow the trajectory of the ball.

Hit-the-Rim Drill

This drill helps develop the lateral precision required in shooting. The player first stands about 4 feet in front of the basket. He is told to hit the front rim as often as possible in the dead center area. As his ability to hit the center of the rim increases, he is moved closer to the free throw line. Oftentimes, we use distances of 4, 8, 12 and 15 feet. Some players gain lateral precision without using the 8- or 12-foot distances. Then the shooter is asked to raise his sights a little.

A common error in this drill is that the shooter will raise his sights too early. He wants to see the ball in the basket. So do I. But I know there are certain shortcuts that cannot be taken. When he satisfies the coach by hitting the rim often enough, it is time to raise the sights and put the ball in the basket.

If the shooter will turn his hand so that the back of it tends to turn toward the mid-line of the body (pronates), the desired spin effect will take place. This tends to soften the shot and deliver the ball, so that a hard and quickly deflecting movement of the ball on the rim is minimized. The ball will stay in a possible entry position longer.

The "I'm Sorry, Coach" Attitude

It is our practice to shoot free throws under varying conditions. First, we practice with players in the lane spaces holding their hands in the air. Secondly, people are invited to attend most practice sessions, and we ask them, at times, to make all the noise they can while we are shooting free throws. Thirdly, a game situation is put on the scoreboard and the shooter is made to win, lose or simulate varying game situations.

Fourthly, we do away with the "I'm sorry, Coach" attitude completely. We know our players are sorry when they miss, so why linger on that attitude? If an arrow can be shot accurately to a bull's-eye by anyone, then we can put a ball of 9 inches diameter into an opening of 18 inches at a distance of 15 feet, even if the 18-inch diameter is 10 feet in the air. The attitude to be desired is eagerness to shoot *with great concentration,* and *to practice day after day after day.* Sure that player who misses is sorry, but we're just not interested in that attitude; we're interested in workers who have rare occasion to be sorry.

Thinking Your Way to Good Free Throw Shooting

Every time a free throw is missed, there is a mechanical flaw which caused it. What a waste of time it is to make that remark.

And yet very few people approach the free throw with that attitude. In fact, shooting is belittled to a degree if shooters refuse to analyze why they miss, when they miss. The problem is to find the flaw. And again, strangely enough, there are many who do not take the time to locate the mechanical error. It can be determined usually if you think about it. It seems stupid or untrue, but most players pay no attention to the missed free throw, either in practice or in games. They just keep shooting, and upon finishing walk away, with the missed shot(s) a forgotten affair.

How did you miss? To the right or to the left? Perhaps I break it down too much for some people, but it is my opinion that precision is a question of right or left. Short or long is a question of force applied. The ability to apply the correct force is a more simple problem than perfecting the flight path of a lateral consideration. A slight deviation of movement of a thumb or a finger, the arm, etc., can cause a missed free throw. A slight error of force applied causes far less missed free throws. This is especially true if the shooter is cautioned to shoot long rather than short, if he has to choose between the two.

In clinics sponsored by the United States Department of State in Panama, Brazil and Spain, I have worked with youngsters from ages six to 18. Most of those kids had far less opportunity to play the game than our young athletes. In those clinics, we demonstrated that a physically normal boy could shoot two out of three free throws *while blindfolded*. All that was done was to orient them for a few minutes as they practiced and before taking the test of three shots. They were told, "A little to the left, a little to the right, stronger, shorter—now you've got it. Now do the same thing three times." I was simply an artillery observer in a Piper Cub using a radio to our artillery people so the guns could be zeroed in. (And if you don't pay attention to the free throw situation, you'll be in the artillery observer's position, but the enemy will be the accurate guns of the alumni.)

On one occasion in Colon, Panama, I was able to work with a young boy about 10 minutes before the clinic started. As the students of the high school gathered, I realized it might be advantageous to start things off with free throws. I called on the lad and he hit two for three right off, while blindfolded. The silence was thunderous in an effect of awe for the boy and the apparent ease with which foul shooting could be executed. Gaining that same awe from your players is half the battle. Forgive what may seem to be a grandiose remark, but any physically normal player can be taught to convert 70% of his free throws if he will listen and try to convert in the ways I have explained.

Good shooting from the free throw line or the floor begets psychological attitudes which bring success. Effective psychological attitudes beget many other desired results. Initially shooting is a physical affair, but it soon becomes a psychological consideration. Some players must be "conned" in a psychological sense, and then the "putting you on" process becomes reality rather than false ego boosting. The shooter now has faith in his shooting ability. That's my objective—deserved faith by the shooter, in himself.

Statistical Analyses of Free Throw Shooting and the Schedule

Some years ago I studied two different styles of free throw shooting, employing primarily a statistical approach. Mr. Irving Langmuir, of the Syracuse University faculty, a statistician of some repute, guided me in the study. It was one of the most meaningful experiences I have had in my preparation to work in the coaching profession.

The study compared two different styles of free throw shooting by college freshmen. They shot 50 free throws per day, excluding holidays, Sundays and days when some individuals missed practice for various reasons. The study was based on shooting done from November 1 of one year and March 10 of the next year. Results were charted on a daily, weekly and monthly plot. The daily, weekly and monthly means were plotted. At this time, the correlation between free throw shooting and making a season's schedule stands out as an important factor. Continued interest in the two styles of shooting has long since ebbed away.

Analyses gave me sound reasons for avoiding tougher opponents on Mondays and possibly Tuesdays. The same indication was apparent for a period of a few days after Christmas vacation. The free throw conversion rate ranged from 55 to 67% in those periods. And since I accept the guiding statement of one study that ". . . 42% of the games could have been won from the free throw line," I have scheduled accordingly ever since. Even if the team is kept together during Christmas, the few days right after that vacation is a good time to stay away from your tougher opponents.

In a country geared to weekend and vacation activities, it doesn't make any difference if your squad is isolated from those activities or not. Just the general atmosphere and attitudes will influence their performance. The author's coaching experience in Latin America proved the study to be inappropriate for that part of the world. The experience contrasted the effects of two different cultures on playing the game in general, and in particular on the free throw phase of the game. Latin American people don't live with any *special* influence for weekends or vacation periods. Perhaps that statement could be debated, but at least their attitude of gaiety, happiness, etc., throughout the week and year, causes less concern for scheduling. In a way it is too bad each week builds up to a Friday-Saturday crescendo in our land—at least for the coach of amateur basketball.

10 • • • • • • •

How to Develop
Good Ball Movement

"If we could move the ball once every two seconds, nothing more would be needed to play winning basketball." This is a statement I have taken from Bruce Drake, former coach of the University of Oklahoma, and possessor of one of the greatest offensive minds I have known. The original "shuffle" he concocted comes as close to such ball movement as any good offensive play I have seen.

The most effective advantage of running a good fast break is not just in beating the opposition down the floor. The good fast break helps develop good ball movement for all phases of offensive play. The drills used to perfect the break are most important because players learn to move the ball accurately and quickly. And isn't good ball movement a most necessary ingredient to run any offensive pattern? It is accurate to say then that drilling the fast break is also building all your other offenses. In fact I have had seasons when we would drill the break but almost never use it, although we like to be ready to run whenever the opportunity comes.

Pointing

"Pointing" means the player's hands must follow the trajectory of the ball for a few seconds after it is released. We insist that

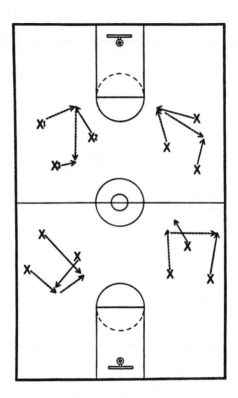

Diagram 10–1. *Three-men-on-the-ball passing drill.*

all our players develop this habit. It is important for the two-hand chest pass as well as the hook pass or any other pass. Players are constantly reminded to follow through and pronate their passing hand(s). Accurate passing is kindred to accurate shooting. I cannot quote any statistics, but I am convinced the accurate passer is apt to be a more accurate shooter—and vice versa. An inaccurate shooter is likely to be a poor passer, and we cannot play our patterns with poor passing.

We open and usually close our practices with passing drills. Diagram 10–1 shows the opening drill, which involves three men rolling and passing the ball between themselves. In the drill, for example, X1 will roll the ball to X2, X2 to X3 and the action continues. The ball should be rolled and passed so that the receiver must move in order to control it. Good receiving ability is a necessary forerunner to good passing; therefore, we feel we have to pay attention to the reception of the ball in all passing drills.

The drill includes a rule which forces a player scooping up the ball from the floor to dribble to the basket for a lay-up, if both he and the ball are moving toward the basket. If neither he nor the ball are moving toward the basket, he may not dribble. We also insist that each ball be controlled with one hand. Two-hand reception is allowed only if the ball cannot be controlled with one hand.

Bounce passes are used in the drill too. The pass should be thrown so as to rebound from the floor rather close to the receiver. The ball should scoot up into the receiver's hands. The high rebounding bounce pass is taboo. That high bounce pass will cause a man driving to break his stride and hinder his drive to the basket.

Finally, all types of passes are utilized, and the drill is used for 5 minutes in our warm-up prior to ball games. I don't agree that it is good policy for a ball club to come out on the floor and start running at even half speed in whatever patterns they may use. A warm-up should be just that, *a warm-up,* and we feel this passing drill does that job too.

In order to do well in this drill, players must be continually on the move. They must meet the ball when receiving it. It is wise to concentrate on developing ability to control the ball as it is rolling on the floor. It's simple to explode from a low-to-the-floor position in order to move for a pass thrown at shoulder level or higher; however, the reverse is not true. Controlling the rolling ball is important in itself, but it also helps establish the habit of playing "low to the floor."

The End-of-Practice Drill

This drill is used by many coaches. However, our teams execute it in a slightly different way, which may be worthy of consideration. Diagram 10–2 shows the five-man weave. If we do not end practice with free throws, we often do so with this drill. Just prior to running it, the squad will have been working on a phase of the game not requiring a lot of physical effort. They have had a "breather." But they also have been through an hour-and-a-half to 2-hour practice. The drill is used, therefore, at a time when fatigue is a factor and we are working on an overload principle for conditioning. Passes thrown under fatigue conditions will help achieve better ball movement in ball games. Once we determine players are ready to play 40 minutes, we don't worry how hard we go in the drill. Obviously it takes a few weeks to get to that point. The drill can also be a rule-of-thumb guide to conditioning. If your squad can run this drill 20 times (round trip counting) at a little better than half speed and at the end of a 2-hour practice, they are ready to play 40 minutes. The high school squad will be able to play 32 minutes if they execute ten round trips after a practice of an hour and a half.

Passes thrown in the drill must be thrown just as accurately when players are tired as when not tired. If it is necessary to slow down to do so, then the pace should be slowed down. If the ball

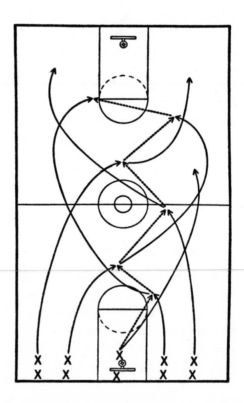

Diagram 10–2. *Five-man weave passing drill.*

can be moved, however, at faster paces, it can be moved accurately at other times when fatigue is less a factor. All players are constantly reminded to throw with confidence and use all types of passes. Receivers get dogmatic attention, as we try to make them know where the ball is and be ready to receive it at any time. The more fatigue they build up, the more demanding we become for accuracy and ball awareness.

Each group of five is allowed to go up and down the floor, seemingly without end. I call the shot on which they can take a break. Release from the drill and practice depends on how long it takes to run the drill efficiently.

The one factor which makes our execution of the drill different possibly than the way others do it is that I often call out the number of passes allowed to go the length of the floor. In effect this dictates the types of passes that can be used. It also regulates the running speed which must be used. If I shout "five," they will be able to run a passing pattern of relatively short passes. If I holler "ten," it will keep them passing the ball longer, slow down their movement and necessitate shorter passes. If I holler "one," someone will have to hustle, all-out, to get up the floor in time. And the pass used in that case undoubtedly will be the baseball pass. If you try this gimmick, you will soon see how easy it is to control the tempo and types of passes thrown.

Mass Shuffle Passing Drill

The mass shuffle passing drill is used about 10 minutes daily during the first two weeks of practice. The squad is placed as in Diagram 10–3. A leader is in front of the group, and whatever movement he makes is imitated by the rest. Players must maintain a good stance and execute movement low to the floor. Four or five people, managers and coaches, walk around the group or in the midst of the players as they throw passes to them. Players continue to follow the movement of the leader, receive the ball when passed near them and pass to a teammate, who will then pass to a coach or a manager. The ball shouldn't be thrown directly to a player but rather to an area in which two or three players can make the reception. This develops quickness in a competitive setting. The original receiver may simply return the

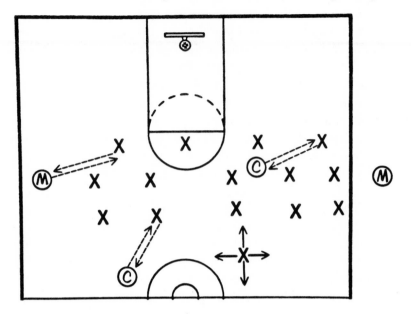

Diagram 10–3. *Mass shuffle passing drill.*

ball to the coach or manager. The idea is to have balls moving all over the place. Heads should be moving, passes thrown with authority and a readiness for both passing and receiving constantly maintained.

Back-of-the-Hand Passing Drill

This drill concentrates on two important phases of ball movement, accuracy and the development of quick hands. The title is somewhat misleading, since we don't throw the ball with the back of the hand but rather receive it on the back of the hand.

Players face a wall and try to hit a designated spot or area on the wall. Passes included in the drill are the baseball pass, bowling ball pass, hook pass, bounce pass, two-hand chest pass and behind-the-back pass. As the player's ability to hit a designated spot increases, the target is made smaller and/or the distance from the wall is increased.

The ball rebounding from the wall is allowed to bounce on the floor, and then the player *must allow the ball to strike the back of one hand.* At this second, the hand is moved as quickly as possible "over the top of the ball" to a position beneath it and

final ball control. This is an extremely difficult drill in the beginning. I still recommend it, however, for younger players as well
as for the more experienced. Slowly the ability to execute the
hand movement will reach the point where the hands will move
fast enough to avoid losing ball control. We use the drill about
3 minutes per practice until the middle of the season, and thereafter as often as needed throughout the season. Many players
seem to enjoy the challenge of the drill and will work with it on
their own time.

Fast Break Passing Drill

Undoubtedly everyone uses this drill or something similar
which will help to develop the fast break game. Although the
bigger men are usually called upon to execute the key pass in the
drill, every player works on the pass often enough to be able to
execute it.

The ball is thrown against the backboard and the players
rebound. As the ball is taken in the air (I don't like to see the
ball hit the floor), the rebounder turns in the air and passes to a

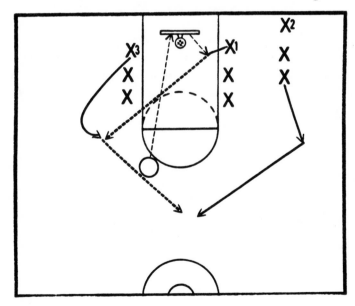

Diagram 10–4. *The fast break passing drill. (Spread
eagle drill.)*

teammate in the first outlet pass area. Diagram 10–4 shows the drill. If the ball is rebounded on the left side, X3 will move to the outlet pass area; X2 will move out if the right side is involved. *We don't want the ball to cross the lane in going to an outlet pass area.* X2 and X3 are forced to move with a turn into the ball and to be on the move, although at a relatively slow pace. If the action involves X3, as in the diagram, then the last man of the X2 line moves to the second outlet pass area. X3 passes to X2. If the ball comes off the board to the right, the process would be reversed of course.

Sometimes the floor is marked with tape to designate the areas wherein the ball is to be received by X2 and X3. The receivers should be moving slowly in those areas, and the passer runs the drill to hit the moving target. *In no case do we want the ball "to be put to the floor."* The baseball pass is used predominantly from the rebounder's spread eagle position. If the players can throw the overhead pass with two hands, they will have achieved a very difficult maneuver. Both passes are difficult to master and ample time must be given to achieve the execution desired.

The Come-up-at-You Passing Drill

The drill is primarily intended to develop a bounce pass which will be used to feed the player on the move; a man driving toward the basket is the prime case. It is a bounce pass which should come off the floor according to the stride of the running receiver. The type of rebound action from the floor *not desired* is:

The type of rebound action from the floor desired is:

The ball should come up into the receiver, which helps him to avoid breaking stride.

Diagram 10–5 shows the drill. The X1 line dribbles as shown and makes a 180-degree jump turn at the end of the dribble. The X2 and X3 lines maintain positions as shown. X1 executes the come-up-at-you pass by sweeping across the top of the ball with his right hand if passing to X2, and with his left hand if passing to X3. The other hand, in each case, supports the ball and is not used in the passing motion.

In the diagram, X1 passes to X2. X2 is the shooter. X1 goes to a corner. X3 rebounds. X3 passes to X1. X1 returns the ball to the middle lane.

While using this drill we tell players the passes they are to use, except for the bounce pass by the middle man. That is not changed. We may shout "bowling pass" and that will be used *in all parts of the drill*, except the pass by the middle man. And, *we want all passes thrown accurately. Not just the feed pass or the pass by the rebounder, but all passes*. It sickens me to see a half-hearted effort made in the return pass to the front. The only time

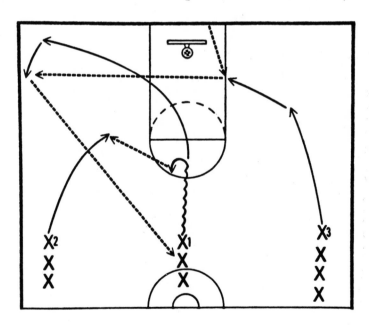

Diagram 10–5. *"The come-up-at-you" passing drill.*

the ball should hit the floor is when the man in the middle is dribbling.

The drill also helps the rebounders to get rebounding shape quickly. And as the ball comes back out to the front line, we are drilling the start of the fast break. At the same time, the start of the drill is the tail-end phase of the fast break situation. Therefore, by using the drill in Diagram 10–4 and this drill, the entire fast break is being put together. Nevertheless, the main reason for putting the drill together is to work on the come-up-at-you pass, and it receives the main stress. This pass is also an excellent delivery for your post men to make to men driving toward the basket.

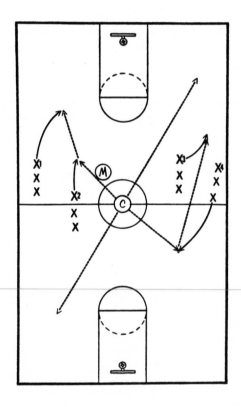

Diagram 10–6. *"Rolling ball" passing drills.*

"Rolling Ball" Passing Drills

In November and December, the "rolling ball" drills are used a great deal. They are taxing physically, and again help to develop passing accuracy as well as good receiving ability. Diagram 10–6 illustrates the drills. The coach is positioned as shown, and a manager is placed so as to help with retrieving and keeping the action alive. A ball is rolled in front of any one of the lines. As the ball is rolled the coach shouts, for example, "back." This means the receiver will pass the ball toward the opposite end of the floor after gaining possession. And it means the front man of an adjacent line will break in a direction away from the ball. Or the coach will shout "front," which indicates the pass will be made in the same direction as the path of the rolling ball. In the latter case, as in the diagram, either X1 or X3 will be the receiver. (This being the case, we have many false starts by a would-be receiver.) All areas of the floor are used. The drill assists in building quick hands and ball release, in addition to the other benefits mentioned.

Lay-Up and Ball Recovery Drill

I know I am very repetitious in saying that quickness is an extremely important factor in playing basketball. I hope I always am, because I want to be a downright bore to our players on the subject. If we can develop speed (movement once in motion) fine, but we must have quickness (the action of getting started). Drilling the recovery of the ball after a lay-up can help build that quickness. Seeing a player shoot and then jog to the end of a line just doesn't appeal to me. We want to have that quickness and determination to change from offense to defense as efficiently as possible. Diagram 10–7 shows the drill which helps us in that regard.

A manager is under the basket and retrieves the ball after each man takes the lay-up. Each player dribbles to the basket, but he must leave the floor without going over a tape marker which is placed about 6 feet from the rim. (The leap should be a combination long and high jump.) Most players can increase their distance both vertically and horizontally, *if they are expected to do so.* As the ball is taken by the manager, he throws it some-

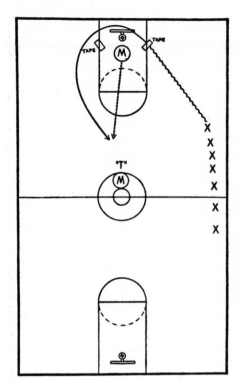

Diagram 10–7.
Lay-up and ball recovery drill. (Half court.)

Diagram 10–8.
Lay-up and ball recovery drill. (Full court.)

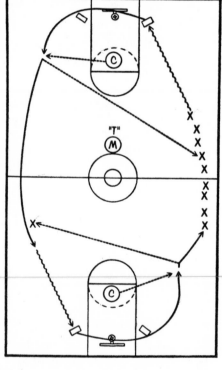

where in the playing area. The player must get it quickly, pass to a teammate in the line and holler that teammate's name just prior to making the pass. He then goes to the line on the other side of the floor.

The pass made by the manager into the playing area is varied constantly. At times, he will fake a pass in one direction and throw in another. This works on quick stops and starts. At other times, the squad is told each player must recover the ball before it bounces three times, twice or just once. This rule really works on the quickness factor. I readily admit also, that I am particularly upset when someone misses the lay-up. At such times, the manager knows he is to throw the ball to the other end of the floor. I then holler "one" (one bounce allowed), and I am pleased to watch the offender scoot along.

This drill also can be fast moving and physically tough. A second person can be used to monitor the action at position "T." His role is to point out unsuccessful execution, correct it and keep people moving. At times we use the whole court for the drill, by having each man use the other basket after his first lay-up and ball recovery. Lay-ups are taken at both ends then. Diagram 10–8 shows the full-court drill. A retriever at both ends would be necessary to run that drill, of course.

We stress accuracy for every pass thrown to people in the lines, and shouting the receivers' names is very important. While the full-court drill is in progress, the monitor in the middle of the floor is really busy. A lot of action should be going on. If it isn't, the fault lies with the manager in charge of conducting the drill.

While the primary objective of this drill is to develop quickness of player and ball movement, other factors are being stressed. It has helped our clubs to break down the lack of talk when we were running predominantly freshmen and sophomore clubs. As mentioned, mental alertness with regard to the ball also creates consciousness, thereby providing impetus to convert effectively from offense to full-court defenses. Accurate long passing is being drilled. The high long jump and lay-up is being perfected. Finally, the middle of the floor coming off the break can be used for the dribble entry and lay-up, as well as the sides.

Five-Man Post Passing Drill

This is a drill I picked out from Clair Bee's repertoire of

passing drills. It is excellent preparation for better ball movement. Five men and a maximum of three balls can be used in running it. Diagram 10–9 illustrates the drill.

X4 and X5 each have a ball. X4 passes to X1, and X5 passes to X1 immediately after X4's pass. X1 may pass to either X2 or X3, but he should turn his head only enough to allow precision passing. For the same reason, all men remain in the same spots as the drill is running. Eventually, X1 will throw the ball accurately without looking.

If X1 passes first to X3, then his second pass would obviously go to X2, and vice versa. X3 and X2 then pass to X4 and X5, respectively. The succession of passes is numbered accordingly— 1, 2, 3, 4, 5, and 6. An important factor in the success of the drill is that X4 and X5 should keep a ball in X1's hands at all times. His head and hands should be working overtime. Proper anticipation by all passers provides maximum hand manipulation for everyone. Then the drill can be made more demanding by using three balls.

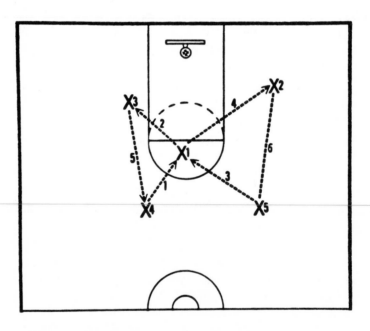

Diagram 10–9. *Five-man   post   passing   drill.   (Two balls.)*

1-on-1, 2-on-2 and 3-on-3 Passing Drills

Although most coaches use these drills, I would be remiss in

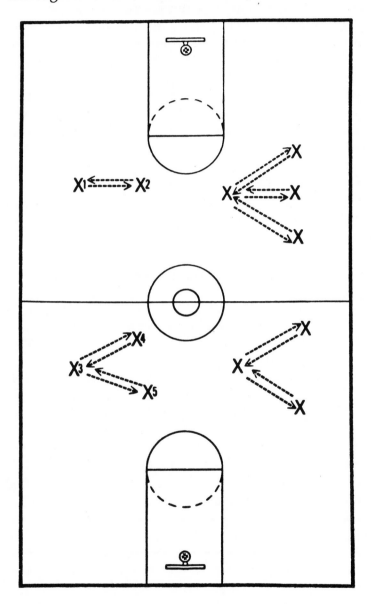

Diagram 10–10. *1-on-1, 2-on-2 and 3-on-3 passing drills.*

not mentioning them since they are a part of our system too. They are simple and very helpful. Diagram 10–10 shows the drills. As we run the drills, we like to remind players "to put a ball in the hands of the receiver as quickly as possible." Intervals of seconds of waiting for a ball detract from the benefits of the drills. We also like to start each man on the 1-on-1 drill and then move him to the 2-on-2 and 3-on-3.

A variation of the drills is used at times. The passers just drop the ball to the side or in front of the receiver. In other words, it isn't passed *to the man.* Quick footwork is now stressed, as well as the concern for quick movement of hands, and ball play continues. I got this idea from watching baseball players drop balls near one another, which called for the hand- and footwork mentioned. A lot of juggling of the ball will sometimes happen in this drill variation. Finally, although the type of pass used will often dictate distances between people, we like to have them from 3 to 6 feet apart. All passes are used nevertheless.

Figure-Eight Under-the-Basket Passing Drill

The drill is used throughout the season for experienced and inexperienced players. It is particularly helpful to younger players because of the basic dance step which must be executed to operate the drill correctly.

Diagram 10–11 depicts the movement of the ball. As the name given the drill indicates, it is performed right in front of the basket. X1 passes to X2. X1 then moves inside of X2. X2 passes to X3, who moves as shown. And the drill continues. The three players can be allowed to run 1 minute or 5 minutes. All types of close-proximity passes are used. The drill develops the handoff type of pass as well as any drill I have used. Moving the ball in heavy traffic is made much more simple by using this drill.

The apparent simplicity of the drill belittles a very important style of movement, and every year we find many college freshmen unable to execute the required footwork upon first engaging in the drill. Sometimes we have found an occasional sophomore unable to do so, which is a self-criticism; no player should escape one season without mastering this footwork. The footwork is executed as illustrated. The place to check for the movement is after a pass has been thrown and the passer is going around the

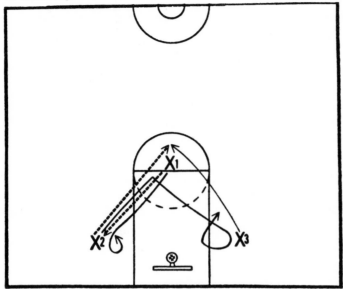

Diagram 10–11. *Figure-eight under-the-basket passing drill.*

outside corner of the pattern. He should not take that corner "merry-go-round" style, but rather with swing steps. He must cut the corner to the inside.

After the pass, the player plants his outside foot as shown and swings the inside foot to the inside. This allows movement, so that he is always looking at the ball. He doesn't run around the corner but cuts it. If combinations of the correct and incorrect movement are executed, the timing of the movement will be thrown off. One man will be too late and one too early. More importantly, poor individual movement will become more habitual.

Many of the passes should be made after faking a shot. Actually, if run in good fashion, the drill is not only a boost to good ball and player movement but also a colorful one to use in pre-game warm-ups.

The 3-on-2 Fast Break Passing Drill

We use this drill about 10 minutes daily. Defensive men are alternated. The X1 line (in Diagram 10–12) is *always filled* by our best ball handlers (guards) and the bigger people fill the outside slots.

Previously, I have said that our fast break is usually drilled in two parts. It is rare that the two parts are put together in practice. And in pre-season scrimmages and actual ball games, I have found this pragmatic effort produces good results. And again, if we can't use the break, this method of drilling helps to cause good ball movement up to the point where we are convinced we can't beat them down the floor.

X1 dribbles as shown. He will dribble until challenged, or if he is not engaged by the defense, he will try to split the defense and go all the way to the basket. If he is challenged, as in the diagram, by O2, he will then stop and pass to the flanker, X2.

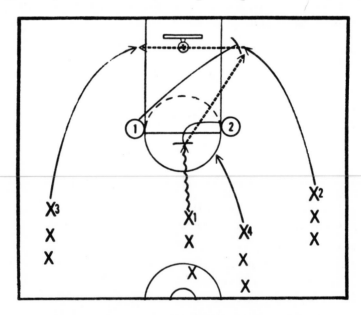

Diagram 10–12. *3-on-2 fast break passing drill.*

O1 usually moves to cover X2 and then the ball would be moved to X3. X4 is the trailer. The trailer should follow X1 on the right-hand side of the middle man. It is the trailer's function to read the situation. If he shouts X1's name, then X1 will automatically bounce pass back to the trailer with his right hand to the right side—always to the right side. X1 would then continue his movement through the defense and many times clears a path to the basket for the trailer. Care should be taken that the flankers (X2 and X3 lines) do not let their momentum take them too deep toward the base line.

Sideline Baseball Pass Drill

This drill is a complement to the drills we use to perfect the "Destroyer Offense," but it works on ball movement which occurs in other phases of other patterns. Diagram 10–13 illustrates the drill.

X2 passes to X1, who moves a few steps toward the X2 line and the center of the floor. X2 receives a return pass from X1 (handoff) after clearing to the outside. X1 then makes a sharp cut off his left foot and drives. X2 takes one more step after receiving the ball, leaps and throws a clothesline pass to X1, who takes the lay-up. X1 goes to the end of the X2 line and X2 to the end of the X1 line.

At the other end of the floor, the drill procedure is reversed by the X3 and X4 lines. X3 takes a step or two toward the basket and X4 passes to him. X4 follows his pass inside and takes the handoff from X3. X3 stops, kicks off the inside foot and drives. X4 leaps from his right foot and clotheslines the ball to X3 with a left-hand baseball pass. In addition to working on the timing of the handoff, both inside and outside, the drill works on tight screening and driving from tight quarters.

Jump Ball Situations

Statistics of our games over the last six years reveal we have had an average of six jump ball situations per game. This means that, in addition to starting each half of the game, there have been four other jump situations. This is very significant informa-

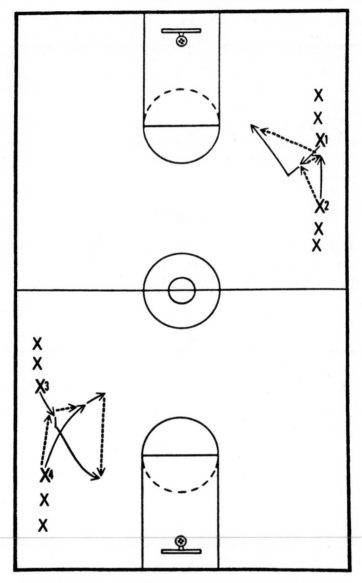

Diagram 10–13. *Inside and outside sideline baseball passing drill.*

tion. First, it is obviously important that we work in some way to help us gain possession a high percentage of times in jump ball battles. Secondly, we want good ball movement after gaining that possession. I have actually seen ball clubs gain possession out of the jump and then wait for the defense to organize. Quite frequently the defense is given enough time to get into a zone press. If you are not blessed with good height (which we are not), you are faced with a real problem. Something must be done to counteract the physical disadvantage.

I must be more dogmatic in my remarks regarding the subject. It is *absolutely vital* to be concerned with jump ball efforts. If the winning or losing spread lies within 24 to 36 points (according to our statistics), it should be worked on. And what team's spread, win or lose, isn't within that range? What I am saying is that if you either win or lose somewhere not in that range (according to our statistics), you will not have to worry about this part of the game. This, I believe, rules out everyone on most occasions.

The Offensive Jump Ball Plan

It's just downright criminal to lose possession in a jump ball fight if you have superior height and/or jumping ability. If we are sure to control the tap we usually want the jumper to use a deep tap to either the sideline or our front court, preferably the former. And before the action takes place, there must be a meeting of the minds between the jumper and all others as to just where the ball will go. The offensive tap situation is shown in Diagram 10–14. X2 and X3 are up fairly tight. The diagram shows the tap going to X4. This being the case, our strong-side guard is to move so that he will be between X4, X1 and perhaps among one or two of the opposition. If the tap falls shorter than we expect, this positioning helps to give us possession; whereas, there would be little chance otherwise. X4 initially moves toward X2. This tends to take the opposition in that direction and gives X4 room to break toward the sideline and usual freedom. X2, the strong-side guard, moves as seen. X3, the weakside guard, takes over the safety man position. X5 comes toward the jump area on the right side.

If X4 gains possession, X2 will continue into the front court and X4 will hit him. If plans reach this point, X4 will fill the left lane, X2 will dribble to the middle, X5 reverses to fill the right

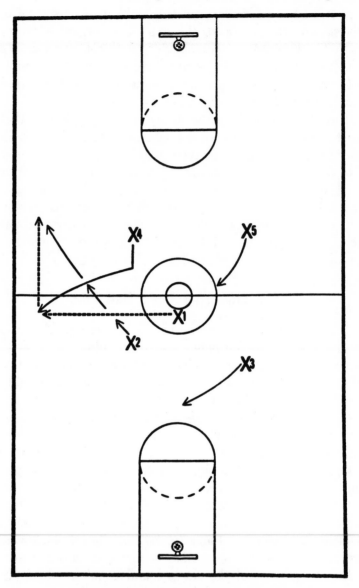

Diagram 10–14. *Offensive jump ball drill.*

lane, X1 will become the trailer and X3 remains the safety man. Diagram 10–15 shows the result.

In drilling the offensive tap, it is simply executed over and over using all five men. Three points are "musts": (1) we want

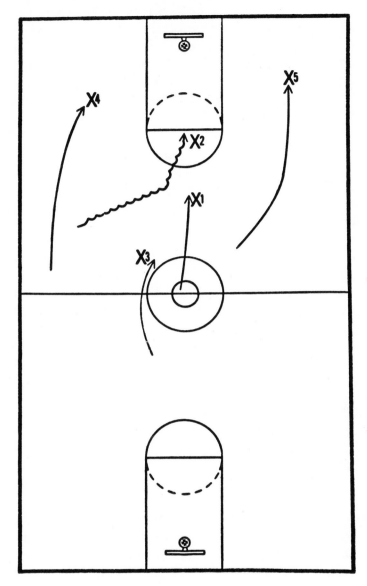

Diagram 10–15. *Continuation of offensive jump ball drill.*

a forward to be the intended receiver (he is usually taller) and preferably in the sideline position; (2) the strong-side guard moves to a position between the intended receiver and the jumper; (3) we want to fast break out of the situation. The drill is sometimes run with the three principal characters, but usually all five men are used. Players are encouraged to practice it with three men before practice, and at other times we drill the three-man arrangement when other individual work is going on. In the event X2 comes up with possession, the only variation will be that X2 will attempt to dribble to the middle immediately.

The Defensive Jump Ball Plan

This situation causes me sleepless nights. I don't think our clubs have done a good job of compensating for the height disadvantage, but perhaps what we try is worth consideration. As a matter of record, I feel Coach Jim Loscutuff of Boston State and formerly of the Boston Celtics, handles jump ball problems as well as any coach I know—especially the defensive tap. He succeeds in offensive taps against our teams, and he also succeeds against superior height. Diagram 10–16 shows our plan to gain possession out of the defensive jump.

I feel it is advantageous to the shorter man to jump in a twisting body motion, which allows him to tap with the outside hand and avoid contact with some part of his taller opponent. Timing his leap correctly will bring that arm and hand to the possible tap without any trouble. This helps the smaller man avoid being muscled out of the play.

The guards are aligned deeper in the back court, and the forwards are tighter to the jump in the front court. Our jumper must provide all the resistance possible, even if there is no way he can control the tap. We figure the tap will most often be made by the right hand of the opponent. Also the flight path will be to his left and to the right of our guards. Therefore, we use a clockwise rotation of men. Each man does so in an "inner-outer" path. It is easier to locate the ball while in flight with an "inside-outside" arc than it is from an "outside-inside" arc. This is similar to most baseball outfielders being more able to come forward than to go backward. X5, in reading the situation, is ready to take a better defensive alignment. X2 should have similar thoughts. The rotation provides movement and coverage on all sides and ultimate defensive balance is quickly gained. Of course, the possibility of

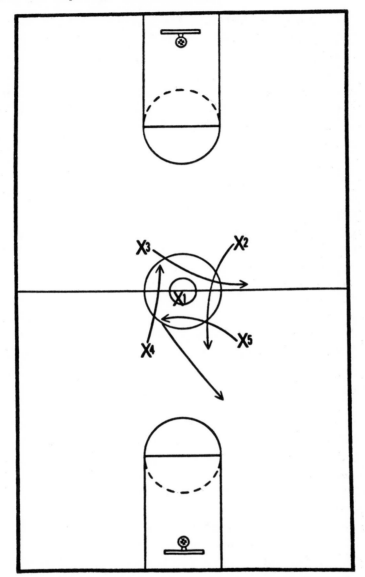

Diagram 10-16. *The defensive jump ball plan.*

gaining possession depends on the timing of the movement as the players rotate through each area. The timing can be drilled by simply setting up the jump situation and having the players try to leap from their movement for the ball. It's a little bit like trying to jump from a slow trot to grab a bird out of the air. As I said, this action causes me sleepless nights.

Finally, if we lose possession, X1 plays ball-you-man defense on the opposing jumper. If he doesn't, the ball can come back to the middle of the floor quickly and your opponent will be looking down your throat with a fast break situation. The ball could go to either side of the floor cleanly since you have moved players close to the jumping area.

The Indefinite Jump Ball Plan

The plan of execution for control of the tap, when it can go either way, is not so different than our defensive jump plan—at least as far as physical movement is concerned. Mentally, the difference should be tremendous. All-out aggressiveness is called for. We still rotate clockwise, but now each man will try to get inside shape on an opponent. In effect, it is a man-to-man effort—and it is a ball-you-man alignment. It's very similar to defensive rebounding. It isn't as important to be thinking of the ball as it is to keep the opposition away from the ball. This again calls for timing. Since the jump will be a battle, we don't expect a long tap to occur with the ball falling closer to the jumpers than in other jump battles.

If inside positions are assumed, it will take a wide tap to give the other club definite possession. And on the other hand, even that is probably denied them since we will have more room to be quick of hand and foot. Diagram 10–17 depicts our effort.

The diagram shows a random alignment. As shown, the rotation matches men. If the opposition overloads any area it will cause a similar overload on our part, but we would still move into inside positions rather than align in them. The match-ups in the diagram would be X2 on O5, X5 on O4, X4 on O3 and X3 on O2. In addition, X1, the jumper, must get between O1 and the ball after the tap is made. As mentioned in the defensive jump ball situation, that quick flip back to the opposing jumper can happen too often to disregard the danger. And again, if it happens, not only does the opponent have possession but good passing lanes and a tailor-made fast break alignment as well.

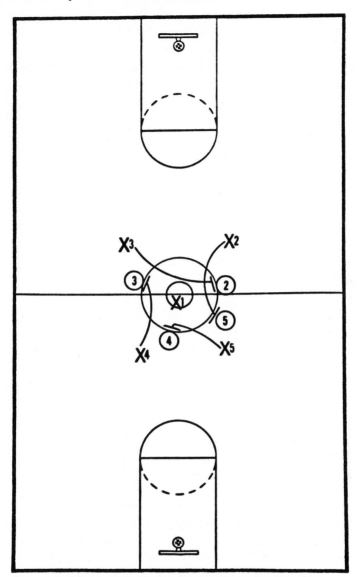

Diagram 10-17. *The indefinite jump ball plan.*

Jump Ball Situations and the Officials

The only caustic comment you will find in this book about officials is in regard to jump ball battles. First, I refuse to worry about the officials. I found very early in my coaching career that I had to have complete faith in them. Perhaps others can, but I am not able to function and survive without that faith. I could not coach, and to any degree officiate too. But there is one phase of the game in which I must be critical of officials. Namely, from a coaching viewpoint, most officials do not toss the ball high enough to allow jumpers to demonstrate their best jumping ability— usually, that is. Secondly, the inconsistency of the height to which the ball is thrown by different officials is prevalent. This lack of consistency causes coaching and execution problems in a crucial part of the game. I realize the difficulties in controlling the inconsistencies, which can be caused by varying player height and even diversifying requests made by coaches for tossing the ball. Putting it in perspective, it is fair for us to be reminded that players shoot at a target which is 10 feet in the air, every time they shoot. Also, we practice almost every imaginable part of the game in order to gain precision. Not so with the official. He has minimal time to practice whatever precision for whatever phase of the game. Nonetheless, despite this display of compassion, it is a rare occasion indeed when I see officials practicing the toss prior to the game. How many times have you witnessed such practice? In the one physical activity calling for precision on the part of the official and which would help players to play the game better, there is evidently little practice effort made.

On the floor of the convention of the National Basketball Coaches' Association in March, 1970, I was one of the coaches asking the Rules Committee to consider having the officials take jurisdiction of the game 30 minutes before game time rather than the previous policy of 10 minutes. It seems to me some of that time could be used to help the officials be more consistent in tossing the ball for jump ball situations. I think, however, that uniformity of the jump ball toss will be the last item in the game to become consistent around the country. The space taken in this book is intended to be helpful to coaches and not to try to dictate to officials.

Pre-Practice Drills

We use a series of drills which are run before practice and

are obviously helpful to the development of good ball movement as well as to other phases of the game. All the drills can be done in 15 minutes, but the squad uses a 20-minute period to do so. This allows for short breaks from the more physically demanding drills and avoids the possibility of incorrect execution because of haste. Most of the drills are used every year, but not all. The drills set up will depend on particular player needs. In other words, a pre-practice drill routine is set up for each player. The drills are put together in an order that meets with the physical condition of each individual in the early season. There have been times when players were ordered to omit all the drills or some of them. We spot-check execution of the drills.

Seven Finger Push-Ups

The title is self explanatory. But the body should be kept level and players should be aware that it may take some time before they can complete the seven push-ups. After being able to do so, an additional work load can be added by having someone place a hand on the back to provide slight resistance to the last three push-ups. It is not our practice to increase the number of repetitions. One minute is all that is needed for this exercise.

Wall-Leg Exercise

This is an effort to work on the anterior part of the upper leg. The player places his back against a wall, flexes his knees and slides down the wall to a semi-sitting position. The position is held about 10 seconds. Five-second rests are given between repetitions. One minute is used to complete four repetitions.

Volleyball Taps

Finger dexterity and good wrist action are helped by this drill. Players work in pairs. The knees should be slightly flexed as the ball is tapped, volleyball style, from player to player. The tap should be made so that it forces the receiver to move to get under the ball. A distance of about 10 feet between players is used. Execution time is 1 minute.

Touching the Rim 30 Times

Every player's jumping ability can be improved. Each man tries to touch the rim from a jumping position in front of the basket. One step is allowed before leaping. If the rim is touched without much effort, we use a height on the backboard which is marked with a piece of tape. Two minutes' time is used.

Reverse Turn Leaps

The drill is used to perfect even 100-degree turns at the end of a dribble. Initially, the drill is run without a ball. If the correct takeoff is troublesome to a player, it is demonstrated and explained in slow motion. When execution is satisfactory, a ball will be used and the turn repeated a number of times in a 2-minute period. The landing should find the player in a "squared," flexed-knee position and looking in the direction from which he came. Half-speed and full-speed approaches to takeoff should be used.

Jump Rebound Drill

This drill does wonders for experienced as well as inexperienced ball players. The rebounder stands in the middle of the lane as the ball is thrown against the board, so that it comes off in a high arc. The player leaps as high as possible, gets possession and brings the ball down hard, in spread-eagle fashion, with the elbows in a protecting position. Two minutes are allowed for the drill, during which time they should be able to bring the ball down about ten times. Hastening the action is taboo, and bringing the ball down with authority should be stressed.

Hop-Skip-Jump Drill

As the title indicates, players hop-skip-jump up and down the floor. Three round trips can be made easily in 1 minute, after the squad is in good physical condition. The drills call for quick starts, changing speeds and leaping ability. All are worthy of attention since they help develop better player movement and therefore better ball movement.

Kangaroo Leap

Six players line up on the base line. They run two round trips in the drill, base line to base line. Feet are kept parallel and the knees are flexed. The arms hang loosely to the side and are hurled forward as the player leaps. We don't try to set any jumping records, but each man should leap about 2½ to 3 feet. Two minutes is ample time to complete the two laps.

Individual Ball Handling Drill

We like to have each player handle the ball daily as he changes body position. The ball should go from one hand to the other, behind the back, between the legs, around the shoulders and up and down the body. The objective is to develop ball handling to the point where movement of the ball is fluid and done unconsciously. Executing the drill an entire season will produce tremendous improvement. Using the drill for a week or two leaves a lot to be desired; prolonged use is a "must."

Scissors Jump

The player is asked to jump 20 times from the usual flexed-knee position as high as possible. As he does so, he spreads his legs laterally or front to rear. Eventually the lateral spread is repeated ten times, and the front-to-rear position is taken ten times. The best format is to alternate the movements. As a variation of the drill, we sometimes have someone throwing a ball to the jumper. The receiver must try to maintain possession if the ball comes at takeoff, in the air or while returning to the floor. Two minutes are ample time to complete the drill.

Theory of Ball Movement

Basketball is a three-man game offensively. It isn't just coincidence that people all over the world play "pickup" games in groups of three. I have seen those "pickup" games in Europe, Latin America and, of course, all over our country. The regulation floor, either high school, college or professional, is comfortably suited for the movement of three players offensively and three defensively. Of course when the entire floor is used, ten people can operate comfortably. But this isn't true in the scoring areas. Unless well-drilled, we often find people standing around while playing in the scoring areas. If the defense is not well drilled in such instance, one or two of its members will be idle when they could be helping others. This happens because of a poorly oriented offensive unit. When both players stand around, the game being played is boring. It develops "too-much-on-the-ball habits." The defensively well-drilled club takes advantage of lack of movement by the offense and defeats them handily. So be it. So, the problem of playing good offensive basketball is concerned with two players who are usually not near the ball. And even that remark is too abrupt. The real "fly in the ointment" is the two defensive men who are allowed to play the helper role by the inactive offensive people. Yes, the two offensive men might hurt you by just getting in the way, but without the two defensive men plugging the gaps, your offense would be in great shape. *Therefore, the problem, from the standpoint of ball movement, is how to keep those two defensive men engaged or involved in the play away from the ball.*

In my opinion, those two men referred to necessitate the use of offensive patterns. Once the patterns are excellently achieved, a free-lance pattern can be advantageous, since the players probably will rely on the strict pattern as a base for their movement anyway.

Therefore, my ideas on ball movement are correctly viewed as taken-for-granted mechanical considerations. We take it for granted the mechanics will be mastered. And if not, those people failing to do so will not play. The mechanics must be mastered in order that the offensive patterns can be better executed than the defensive patterns used against them. Both phases will probably be concocted by the coach, either as he adapts his ideas to ones already tested or, occasionally, when he comes up with something new. But the player must assume the willingness to master the mechanical phases involved with ball movement. The degree of mastery of those mechanics dictates the level of play in which each player finds himself. The correct attitude in practicing is the first quality of character I look for when recruiting.

Utopia is that the coach can take it for granted his players have, or will master, the mechanics. And that is dangerous. It is at that point that the coach's way of installing a prevailing discipline will dictate the degree of success which will be achieved. Mastery of fundamentals cannot be left to chance. But it is wiser psychologically to develop player responsibility for that mastery than for the coach to accept the same responsibility every day in practice. However, the perspective I have in mind is that a coach should dream. And he does well to dream of patterns, if he has instilled the psychology among his players which will perfect the fundamentals.

The offensive patterns which should be executed and made possible by mechanical mastery, must be tested in actual game conditions before they can be completely reliable—not once or twice, but a number of times. Perhaps they should be tested over an entire season. I really feel a disastrous error is sometimes made when a coach abandons a certain phase of his game just because things aren't going too well on a given night. So many factors can be involved which detract from true testing of his ideas, that it is wise to look the situation over with considerable retrospect. This is why "tis no sin to imitate." What has been successful for others probably, to a fairly reliable degree, will be successful for us. Why waste time testing new ideas when there are those already available which will succeed?

Let me ask you a question: How many new offensive ideas have you picked up in the last two years; in the last five or ten years? Probably few. This doesn't necessarily mean offensive innovations which would be good for the game don't exist, but probably that we are imitating too much or not thinking enough. *The real all-American champion, in the best tradition of the American champion, is that team well-drilled in tested patterns of an imaginative and discerning coach.* This coach is *discerning,* as he accepts styles of play best suited to his system, *imaginative* because he has blended new ideas into the old. And this is the usual formula for success in coaching basketball on any level.

Index

A

Adjustments:
  continued pressure "up the line," 54
  defensive, 55
  major, without, 31
  relieving back line pressure, 123
Aggressiveness, 95
Alignment:
  adjustments, 31
  against full-court zone press after field
    goal, 31
  around the corner, 38, 39
  "ball you man," 34, 48, 55
  counteracting zone presses, 34
  defensive free throw, 164-165
  depth up the floor, 30
  "Destroyer Set," 59, 60
  diagonal line principle, 30
  Double, 47, 48
  drilling, 30
  5-on-5 arrangement, 34
  four-man back line, 53
  "getting to the alignment," 30, 32
    after gaining possession via turn-
      over, 32
    part of alignment, 30
  half-court zone presses from base line,
    against, 36-38
    achieving best results, 36
    diagram, 37
    drills, 36, 38
    minimizes problem of alignment,
      36
    two-hand over-the-head pass, 38
  left-handers, 32, 36, 38-39 (*see also*
    Left-handers)
  long baseball pass, 30, 31
  mid-court zone press, against, 34-36
    diagram, 34
    pleasant to work, 35
  one-half diamond-two defense, 137
  1-on-1 situation, 34, 38, 51

Alignment (*Cont'd.*)
  1-2-2 traditional but trapping zone,
    135
  random situations, drill, 34
  random turnover situation, 32, 33, 34
  same against all zone presses, 30
  shoulder, 94, 98
  three-quarter court zone press, against,
    35-36
    decrease angle between X1 and re-
      ceiver, 35-36
    diagram, 35
    engage the defense, 36
    long pass, 36
  three-quarter floor, 123
  3-2 mid-court zone press, 145
  2-on-2 situation, 34
  2-2-1 zone press, 129
  zone presses, 113
Alterations, fit to personnel and ideas, 58
Arold, Paul, 86
Around the corner, 38, 39, 61

B

Background, 22-23
Back line pressure, relieving, 119-123,
  124
Back-of-hand passing drill, 180
Ball movement, 23-24, 175-207
"Ball you man," 34, 48, 55, 59
Base line, 94
Baseball pass, 23, 24-26
"Blaze," 90
Bounce pass, 116
"Break back," 51, 53
"Burn," 90

C

Cat-and-mouse option drill, 71, 78-79
Chamberlain, Wilt, 86
Clubs, ball, 58
Coaches, 46

Come-up-at-you passing drill, 182-184
Conversion:
   "Destroyer Set" to defense, 79-82 (*see also* "Destroyer Set"*)
   offense to defense, 86-90, 92-93
Corner trapping, 131

D

Defense (*see* Man-to-man defense)
Defensive changes:
   conversion from offense to defense, 86-90, 92-93
   systematic defensive variation, 90-92
Destroyer, Rule #7, Section #6, (b), 42
"Destroyer Set":
   ability to beat pressing defenses, 58
   against teams with greater height, 58, 80, 81
   alignment, 59, 60
   alterations of offense, 58
   ball-you-man defenses, 59
   basic premise, 58
   combat fast-breaking ball clubs, 58
   conversion to defense, 79-82
     areas where shots taken, predict, 80
     attack when possession lost, 80
     defense as attack situation, 79
     how ball comes off board, 80
     man-to-man defense, 80
     no defensive calls from bench, 80
     opposition using three guards, 82
     possession through defensive measures, 81
     quickness and vigorous action, 81
     shot missed by guard, 80
     shot missed by post man, 80-81
     tip-in, 81
     turnover, 82
   defensive man must *react*, 59
   drills to implement, 74-79
     cat-and-mouse option, 71, 78-79
     double block option, 77
     pick-and-roll, 75-76
   Durkee, Jim, 63
   execution, 59-71
     "around the corner," 61
     double screen, 64, 68
     drive series in cleared-out area, 68
     expediency, 62
     first movement, 59, 60
     fluidity, 68

"Destroyer Set" (*Cont'd.*)
   inside arc movement, 63
   inside-hand bounce pass, 63
   isolating to play 1-on-1, 68-70
   low post penetration, 64
   over-the-head two-handed pass, 62
   passing lanes, 62
   "pick and roll" play, 62, 63, 71
   screening efforts, 66, 68
   short jumper, 62
   slough situation, 68
   step-out pass, 66
   take shot quickly, 63
   guard around series, 72
   high and low post play, 58
   how it can help, 57
   impossible to jam middle, 58
   Krug, Jim, 57
   lane stack offense, 56-57, 59
   Lincoln, Jim, 68
   McAllister, Carl, 57
   offense can determine tempo, 59
   offensive board area, 56
   offensive man *acts*, 59
   offensive rebounding strengthened, 57
   offensive thrusts, 57
   1-on-1 basketball, 58
   1-on-1 play executed easily, 57
   only threat are zone presses, 58
   or "Double," 57
   Owens, Ted, 61
   perfecting, 72, 74
   player runs every position, 72, 74
   protection for every pass thrown, 57
   Russell, Bob, 68, 72, 74
   talent requirements, 59
   Tipson, Bob, 57
   X5, tallest player, 59
   zone presses neutralized, 58, 59
Diagonal line principle, 30
Double alignment, 47, 48
Double block option, 77
"Double" offense (*see* "Destroyer Set")
Double screen, 64, 68
Drake, Bruce, 141, 142
Drill:
   "back break," 51, 53
   back-of-hand passing, 180
   basic offense, 45
   cat-and-mouse option, 71, 78-79
   come-up-at-you passing, 182-184

Drill (*Cont'd.*)

conversion from offense to defense, 89, 91

counteracting zone presses, 34

double block option, 77

effective rebounding, 151-165 (*see also* Rebounding)

end-of-practice, 177-179

fast break passing, 181-182

15-minute passing, 25

figure-eight under-the-basket passing, 190-192

five-man post passing, 187-188

5-on-5 arrangement, 34

half-court zone presses from base line, against, 36, 38

hit the rim, 170-171

hop-skip-jump, 204

interchange from standstill position, 53

jump rebound, 204

kangaroo leap, 205

lay-up and ball recovery, 185-187

left-handers, 36

mass shuffle passing, 179-180

mid-court passing, 27

1-on-1 situation, 34, 100

1-on-1, 2-on-2, 3-on-3 passing, 189-190

passing, 25, 55

pick-and-roll, 75-76

player runs every position, 72, 74

preparatory, 25-28

pre-practice, 202-205

random situations, 34

relieving back line pressure, 123

reverse turn leaps, 204

"rolling ball," 185

scissors jump, 205

seven finger push-ups, 203

"shutting off the honey," 129

sideline baseball pass, 193

sideline interchange, 51, 53 (*see also* Execution)

sideline pressure, 48, 50

sideline receiving, 27

3-on-3, 100-102

3-on-2 fast break passing, 192-193

touching the rim 30 times, 204

trapping, 119

12 ball players, 51

two-hand chest pass, 25

Drill (*Cont'd.*)

two-hand over-the-head pass, 25, 38

2-on-2 situation, 34, 100

volleyball taps, 203

wall-leg exercise, 203

weakside drive defensive, 109-111

Durkee, Jim, 63

E

End-of-practice drill, 177-179

Execution:

adjustment to continued pressure "up the line," 54

Destroyer, Rule #7, Section #6 (b), 42

"Destroyer Set," 59-71 (*see also* "Destroyer Set")

first movement of offense, 44-48

ball-you-man alignment, 48, 55

basic alignment of Double Offense, 48

basic offense drill, 44, 45

basis for entire offense, 44

coaches, 46

complete offense without variation, 47

defense's efforts to counteract, 44

defense may duplicate offensive maneuvering, 44

"Destroyer" offense into Double alignment, 47

distances of passes, 45-46

effective defensive action, 46

illustrated, 44

never losing possession, 46

player experienced in all positions, 46

reaction to sideline pressure, 50

reception over out-of-bounds area, 44

return movement, 48

sideline interchange, 49

sideline pressure drill, 48, 50

first pass, 42

guard positions, 42

height, 42, 55

mental attitude, 41, 42

moving toward ball in receiving, 42

one type of pass, 41

panic of defense, 55

passing drills, 55

patterned offenses, 51

Execution (*Cont'd.*)
percentage shot, 42
sideline interchange drill, 51, 53
"break back," 51, 53
diagram, 52
four-man back line alignment, 53
indefensible basic offensive principle, 51
interchange from standstill positions, 53
"me," 53
1-on-1 alignment, 51
out-of-bounds pass, 51
trap situation, 53
two-man front, defense, 51
skepticism, 41
speed, 42, 55
tempo, 41
terminology, 41
3-on-3 situation, 51
3-2 three-quarter court zone press, against, 51
variations, 55

F

Fast break passing drill, 181-182
Feed pass, defensing, 104-105
15-minute passing drill, 26
Figure-eight under-the-basket passing drill, 190-192
"Fire," 90
Five-man post passing drill, 187-188
5-on-5 arrangement, 34
5-on-5 rebounding drill, 159-160
"Flat," 90
"Flat" front line pressing zone, 116
Fluidity, "Destroyer Set," 68
Fouling, 58, 155-156
Four-man back line alignment, 53
Free throw shooting:
attitude, 171
body mechanics, 167-168
hit-the-rim drill, 170-171
practice timetable, 169-170
season's plan, 168-169
statistical analyses, 173-174
thinking, 171-173

G

"Getting to the alignment," 30, 32
Guard around series, 72
Guard positions, 42

H

Half-court zone presses from base line, 36-38 (*see also* Alignment)
Half-diamond-two, 90
Height, 42, 55, 58, 80, 81, 152-153
"Helping defenses," 95
Hip movement, 96
Hit-the-rim drill, 170-171
"Honey," 125
Hop-skip-jump drill, 204

I

Inside arc movement, 63
Inside-hand bounce pass, 63

J

Jabbar, 86
Jump ball situations, 193-202
Jump rebound drill, 204
Jump shot, 153

K

Kangaroo leap, 205
Krug, Jim, 57

L

Lane stack offense, 56-57, 59
Lay-up, 153
Lay-up and ball recovery drill, 185-187
Left-handers:
against half-court zone presses from base line, 36, 38
around the corner against pressure zone, 39
ball handling ability, 38
drills, 36
height, 38, 39
over-the-head pass, 38
sideline, 32
sideline ball movement pattern, 39
three on team, 38
Lincoln, Jim, 68
Lob pass, 116
Long baseball pass, 30, 31
Long pass, 36
Low post penetration, 64

M

Man-to-man defense:
ability to execute few basic ideas, 96
aggressiveness, 95

Man-to-man defense (*Cont'd.*)
  base line, 94
  concentration, 94
  conditioning, 96
  defense must attack, 96
  defensive stance, 96
  defensive talk, 97
  eyes on opponent's belt line, 96
  feed pass, 95, 104-105
  "helping defenses," 95
  hip movement, 96
  holler "shot," 96
  hustle, 96
  individual fundamentals, 96
  "off the ball," 97, 99
  "okay," 99
  "on the ball," 97
  1-on-1, 95, 97, 100
  "over the top," 99
  post, 102-104
  pride, 96
  shoulder alignment, 94, 98
  sliding, 99
  "sloughing," 95
  "strong side," 97
  "switching," 95
  3-on-3 drills, 101-102
  2-on-2 drills, 100
  "weak side," 97
  weakside drive, 105-109
  weakside drive defensive drill, 109-111
Mass shuffle passing drill, 179-180
McAllister, Carl, 57
"Me," 53
Mid-court zone press, 34-36 (*see also* Alignment)
"Mike" offense, 90
"Mine," 86
Movement, ball, 23-24, 175-207

N

National Collegiate Athletic Association, 21

O

"Off the ball," 97
Offense to defense, conversion, 86-90, 92-93
"Okay," 99
"On the ball," 97, 113

One-half diamond-two defense:
  "back door" play, 141
  ball to floor a great deal, 143
  basic alignment, 137
  beginning movement, 138
  best rebounder, 137
  deep switch, 139
  diagrams, 140, 141, 142, 143, 144
  Drake, Bruce, 141, 142
  guards, 139
  guidelines, 140
  man-to-man action by guards, 137
  overload, 139, 140, 142
  "shuffle," 141
  teams against which effective, 137
  weakside force-pass situation, 142
  zone execution by bigger people, 137
One-hand push shot, 154
1-on-1 passing drill, 189-190
1-on-1 situation, 34, 38, 51, 57, 58, 68-70, 95, 97, 100
1-2-2, 90, 112
1-2-2 traditional but trapping zone, 135-137
1-2-2 zone press, 123-125 (*see also* Zone presses)
Out-of-bounds pass, 51
Out-of-bounds play, defensing, 154
Overload situation, 136, 137, 139, 140, 142
Over-the-head pass, 38
Over-the-head two-handed pass, 62
"Over the top," 99
Owens, Ted, 61

P

Passes:
  baseball, 23, 24-26
  bounce, 116
  distances increase, 45-46
  first one, 42
  inside-hand bounce, 63
  lob, 116, 123
  long, 36
  long baseball, 30, 31
  one type, 41
  out-of-bounds, 51
  over-the-head, 38
  over-the-head two-handed, 62
  protection, 57
  sideline, 25
  step-out, 66

Passes (*Cont'd.*)
two-hand chest, 25
two-hand over-the-head, 25, 38
Passing drills, 55
Passing lanes, 62
Percentage shot, 42
Physical attributes, 42, 55
Pick-and-roll drill, 75-76
"Pick and roll" play, 62, 63, 71
"Point," 90
Pointing, 175
Post, defensing, 102-104
Post man shooting, 154

R

Random turnover situation, 32, 33, 34
Rebounding:
big man, 152-153
drills, 157-164
defensive, 157-159
5-on-5, 159-160
head-to-head defensive, 162-164
"tiger," 161-162
from defensive free throw alignment, 164-165
jump shot, 153
lay-up, 153
offensive, strengthened, 57
one-hand push shot, 154
out-of-bounds play, 154
post man shooting, 154
rule change and fouling, 155-156
sequel to practice rule change, 156-157
team, 155
theory and reality, 165
trailer play in fast break, 154-155
Receiving, moving toward ball, 42
"Red," 90
Reverse turn leaps, 204
"Rolling ball" drills, 185
"Ruby," 90
Rule #7, Section #6, (b), 42
Russell, Bob, 68, 72, 74, 86

S

Scissors jump, 205
Score, predicting before game, 113-114
Screening efforts, 66, 68
Seven finger push-ups, 203
"Shot," holler, 96
Shoulder alignment, 94, 98

Shutting off the "honey," 125-129
"Shutting off the honey" drill, 129
Sideline baseball pass drill, 193
Sideline interchange, 49
Sideline interchange drill, 51, 53 (*see also* Execution)
Sideline pass, 25
Sideline pressure, reaction, 50
Sliding, 99
Slough situation, 68
"Sloughing," 95
Slow-down basketball, 114
Speed, 42, 55
Stance, defensive, 96
Step-out passes, 66
"Strong side," 97
"Switching," 95

T

Talent requirements, 59
Talk, defensive, 97
Tempo, 41
Terminology, 41
"Three," 90
3-on-3 drills, 100-102
3-on-3 passing drill, 189-190
3-on-3 situation, 51, 100-102
3-on-2 fast break passing drill, 192-193
Three-quarter court zone press, 35-36
3-2, 90
3-2 mid-court zone press:
alignment, 145, 146
diagrams, 145, 146, 147
start of movement, 145
3-2 three-quarter court zone press, against, 51
"Tiger drill," 161-162
Tip-in, 81
Tipson, Bob, 57
Trailer play, fast break, 154-155
Trap situation, 53
Trapping, zone presses, 114-119 (*see also* Zone presses)
Turnover, 32, 33, 34, 82, 113
Two-hand chest pass, 25
Two-hand over-the-head pass, 25, 38
Two-man front, 51
2-on-2 passing drill, 189-190
2-on-2 situation, 34, 100
2-2-1, 90, 116, 129-135 (*see also* Zone presses)

V

Variations, 55
Volleyball taps, 203

W

Wall-leg exercise, 203
"Weak side," 97
Weakside drive:
   defensing, 105-109
   drill, 109-111
Weakside force-pass situation, 142

Z

Zone presses:
   alignment, 113
   offense "on the ball," 113
   one-half diamond-two defense, 137-145 (*see also* One-half diamond-two defense)
   1-2-2, 112, 113, 123-125

Zone presses (*Cont'd.*)
   1-2-2 traditional but trapping zone, 135-137
   predicting score before game, 113-114
   relieving back line pressure, 119-123, 124
   shutting off the "honey," 125-129
   take away a running game, 113
   3-2 mid-court, 145-147 (*see also* 3-2 mid-court zone press)
   trapping, 114-119
   turnovers, 113
   2-2-1, 129-135
      alignment, 129, 130
      corner trapping, 131
      diagrams, 132, 133, 134
      forced to show hand, 135
      movement into traps, 129
      point action up front, 129
      use, 129
   typical defensive game plan, 113